MY MOMMA DONE TOLD ME

Behave yourself and remember whom you belong to. If you lie down with dogs, you get up with fleas. Birds of a feather flock together. People judge you by the company you keep. What will the neighbors think? Good girls don't talk like that. No time to do it right, just time to do it over. It's the poor dryer that can't help the washer. Shut the door. Were you raised in a barn? Spare the rod; spoil the child. Children should be seen and not heard. If I told you once, then I've told you a thousand times. I'd be thinner and a little shorter. When it mattered, I wanted to be thinner. I'd change the sagging of my body that is happening as I'm getting older. I'd change my feet. I hate my toes. I would have fuller lips and thicker eyelashes. I'd be like Ruth Lovely—she's as good as she is beautiful. I wouldn't change anything. I'm quite satisfied with what God gave me. Yep, I have a regret! I regret that I married the wrong person. I have some regrets. It's hard to say that things didn't turn out like I planned because I never had any definite plans for my life. I always wanted to be married, have children and a home. I had to wear dresses and ruffled socks and ruffled underwear. I wore Mary Jane's, a hand-smocked pinafore and a bow in my hair. My cousins wore little suits. We looked like dolls they looked like grownups. No, my mother didn't make a difference. She told us she was an equal opportunity ass whooper. She'd whip us all. They treated us equally. My mother and father dealt with us the same. He always got off lighter and had more freedom. I felt stifled in that way. I can't say there was a difference in the way we were disciplined. The Queen says the things we wish we could! Why are dogs men's best friends? I'm a girl and my dog Snow is my best friend! My goodness, what will they think? How will it make your family look? What about your reputation?

To read more sayings and interview notes not included in the book turn to the last page.

Live a POWERFUL Life

How to Move Beyond Pleaser and Good Little Girl to Conscious Queen

Live a POWERFUL Life

Allyn Evans

How to Move Beyond Pleaser and Good Little Girl to Conscious Queen

Allyn Mitchell Evans
www.allynmitchellevans.com

Live a Powerful Life:
How to Move Beyond Pleaser and Good Little Girl to Conscious Queen

©Allyn Mitchell Evans 2023

ISBN-13: 978-1-45055-819-8
ISBN-10: 1-45055-819-4
Library of Congress Number
LCCN: 2010903210

Edited by Donna Warner and Carolyn Howard-Johnson
Cover design by George Weiss of Tekeme Studios

Be Extraordinary
Publishing

Published in 2005 by Star Publish (Grab the Queen Power: Live Your Best Life!). Republished in 2010 by Create Space. Republished in 2024 by Amazon Publishing Service.

Printed in the United States of America

DEDICATION

To my father, Ned Alan Mitchell, who taught me to reach for the stars, and to my mother, Bettye Branch Mitchell, who, understanding how much I wanted to be Queen, did everything she could to help me become one. Thank you for the support and encouragement that has nourished me always. The steps you've taken ahead of me will forever brighten my path.

To my grandmother, my Mama Doyce, who inspired me years ago by confidently penning her own story.

CONTENTS

A PARABLE

NCE UPON A time, there was a Princess destined to be Queen. Disturbed by the child's wild nature, the Queen and King fretted over what to do about her. The two Highnesses had never experienced anything like this child—boisterous, independent and opinionated. These traits would not do. The King spent hours on end asking his God why He had made this child a Princess instead of a Prince. His little Princess arrived in the Kingdom much more suited to be King. Alas, being a future Queen who acted kingly could not be permitted, or surely the Kingdom would topple!

Faced with the momentous task of making sure the Princess would fulfill her destiny, the Queen Mother and King Father relied on their Royal Advisors—three highly ranked officials within the royal system.

The Queen Mother dreaded the day when all would be different, and when her little girl would forever be changed. She also knew she must do nothing to stop it. Daily in the chapel, the Queen Mother fussed at her God. "Why did You send me a child that needs fixing? Why? Why do you punish my child with my own failings?"

No matter what the cause, it was apparent to everyone, including the Queen and King, their little Princess did not act very queenly. She must be righted.

On her very next birthday, all the court assembled. The Trumpeter trumpeted and the Court Announcer announced.

"Your Royal Highnesses today marks the fifth birthday of your daughter, the Royal Princess. Today her evaluation shall begin."

Trumpets again resounded. Members of the royal court cheered. Flanking each side of the small Princess, the King and Queen escorted their daughter to her challenge.

In the first room, the Princess found Countess Corridor. The Countess, recognized for her innate ability to Accurately Judge Appropriate Versus Inappropriate Behavior Befitting a Queen, observed the Princess as she played with other royal children. The task took three hours. She returned the child to the next room. All eyes were fixed upon her. She merely looked away, with only a sad little shake of her head.

In the second room, the Princess found Prince Scarlet. The Prince, recognized for his innate ability to Interpret Unspoken Societal Rules and Ethics, talked to the Princess. His evaluation took another three hours. After completing his exam, he mumbled to Countess Corridor about the impossibility of it all.

In the third room, the Princess found Countess Pride. The Countess, recognized for her innate ability to Instill Self Importance, tested the Princess. These tests also went on for three, grueling hours. Dumbfounded by what she learned; Countess Pride demanded a meeting with the others.

The next day, amid the sound of trumpets, the three highly ranked officials presented a Royal Proclamation to the Queen and King.

Countess Pride stepped forward. "Your Highnesses. It is with much regret that I report on the situation. All of us agree that in order for your little Princess to succeed, she needs much, much work. As Royal Servants to the Kingdom, we all pledge our undivided attention and will work diligently with your daughter."

The other two solemnly nodded in agreement.

The Countess continued her speech. "We require ten years to work with your daughter. It is our contention that your daughter should be removed to a separate wing of the Kingdom so as not to be influenced by you. We would like to begin our training immediately. Your Highnesses, do you approve?"

The Queen ducked her head to mask the tears. As it had happened to her, so it must happen to her child. The King moaned loudly. In a loud commanding voice he proclaimed, "Make it so."

Countess Corridor offered her hand to the child. The Princess, enjoying their time together so far, eagerly joined the Countess. The Queen

Mother held her head high, demonstrating to all subjects her belief in the Customs of the Kingdom. The King buried deep his own sadness. He bid his only daughter farewell…

To read the rest of the parable, turn to page 203.

Bound By Tradition

I picture my great grandmother wrapped in a straight jacket. She was not crazy. She was bound. So bound by the traditions and rules of society she couldn't be herself. In my vision, I see her expectantly entering marriage only to be beaten down by expectations, by life. Marriage sucked the spirit right out of her, took away her joy and pushed her to the very edges of sanity. Great grandfather was not the boogey man. He was a good man. Through no fault of his own, he was what society had created. His "society" was accepted by all the others—all the well-meaning friends, family and neighbors that demanded she act and behave in a certain way. In this place, there were no double standards. All conformed and played by the rules. The saddest part is that the participants never questioned the rules, or if the game was fair. My great grandmother was no different. She never questioned. Instead, she demanded that all in her charge play too. She believed every word, gave the culture power to control her and then passed all she learned to the ones that followed.

—Olivia, 40 years old

The women who came before me faced a similar struggle. Starting years before my great grandmothers' time, each generation broke free, if only by a little…altering the experiences of those who followed.

INTRODUCTION

---◦◦◦---

Who Am I?

I am a woman bound by tradition.

—Crouching Tiger

Excerpt from My Journal—

Tonight I was so angry with my daughter. Addy just was not acting right. She whined, wouldn't say "yes, ma'am," "no ma'am." That child would not mind her manners. She was thinking only of herself. Selfish. That's it; she was being selfish. Very embarrassing. I should have more control. My parents certainly had control over me when I was her age. I knew how to act.

Upstairs in the bathroom, I turned her around to face me. I dropped down on my knees, gripped her shoulders, and looked her straight in the eyes. I really let her have it. "Addy Evans," I said at the end of my tirade, "you must always put others before yourself. Always!"

Then I gasped. This was the message I had spent years trying to overcome, the one I felt was the root of my own problems. I started laughing. And, then I started to cry.

HEN I WAS younger, I often heard I was too loud, too pushy, and too dominant. Hardheaded. I grew up in Mississippi. In the South, pushy was not an esteemed quality in girls. Just look at Scarlett O'Hara...alone, unloved, with only her determination to rebuild her childhood home to sustain her. Desiring approval and love, I reached the conclusion I needed to be different; hardheaded was not a good thing.

I learned to keep my voice soft and my opinions to myself, since my opinions usually conflicted with the ones voiced around me.

I wasn't alone in absorbing this message.

Sela Ward, also from Mississippi, says in her book, *Homesick,* "I was the perfect young Southern woman: quiet, demure, feminine, seen and rarely heard. Polite. Proper. Never raised my voice. Never gave my parents a moment's trouble. Shied away from unpleasantness. Strove to maintain that teeth-together-lips-apart ideal." She, too, hid her true self.

In *You Own the Power,* Rosemary Altea explained the message she received while growing up: "Be quiet, wear a mask, stay in the shadows, keep a low profile, pretend to be somebody else."

Donning my own mask, striving to be polite and proper, quiet and demure, I developed a modus operandi expressed by the following mantra: What will others think? I applied this question to each individual I met. My years of programming taught me to instinctively determine what other people needed or wanted from me. Since I had figured out being me wasn't good enough, I would be whoever *you* (and you, and you, and you) wanted me to be. I took my programming even a step further. I would be just like you. It seemed to work. People liked me. They wanted to be with me.

Except when my new way of being backfired. With my real self tucked away, I ended up frustrated and angry. Buried anger doesn't remain buried. In my adolescent years, Little Miss Nice disappeared, and Miss Naughty peeked out. My anger birthed a mean streak. Because I couldn't articulate my feelings, I buried my true self much, much deeper. I came to hate the person I was. I was disgusted by my out-of-control behavior and figured that everyone else must be, too.

The turmoil took on a physical aspect. I battled stomach ailments and severe acne. During those 'crazy' years, I made at least one trip to the hospital due to a most severe spastic colon attack.

The stomach complications or spastic colon, and the acne plagued me into my thirties. And while I was able to clamp down on Miss Naughty as I grew older, I couldn't quite make Miss Nice fit the same way anymore. For the first fifteen years of my adulthood, even with a good husband and lots of opportunities, I was filled with a sadness and longing, and a hunger that pushed me to search without knowing what I was looking for. About all I knew was I didn't want what I had grown up with. I wanted something different. Without a cultural precedence or role models, it was up to me to discover what that something was. Sue Monk Kidd, author of *The Dance of the Dissident Daughter,* could have been speaking for me when she wrote, "When we start this journey, we discover a couple of things right away. First, the way is largely uncharted, and second, we're all we've got."

In the beginning of my own exploration, I imagined my discontent stemmed from my failure to find meaningful work. I continued with my formal education, and began reading widely in the 'selecting the right career' field. My formal education, first psychology and then an MBA, gave me good skills, but none that translated into my right livelihood. I thought my dissatisfaction came from the lack of money and prestige. I couldn't find the job that met my financial needs or acknowledged the value of my abilities. My informal education helped me realize before I knew what I had to offer and what the world had to offer me, I needed to know myself. I had to go back for that self I had buried so many years ago. I had to recognize the messages that compelled me to deny that self, and learn a new language that would invite her to take her rightful place in the light.

Along the way, I had a baby. My daughter Addy presented me with even greater incentives. I needed to help provide for her financially, and I wanted to be with her as much as possible. It took me three years, but I finally made it happen. I became a stay-at-home mother with a part-time job. I was living the life I had *never* wanted to live. I was happier than I had ever been.

For the next two years, I earned my share of our family's income with home-based business ventures. But when Addy was old enough to go to school full-time, I was ready to follow my heart as I made my own way in the world. The trouble was I still didn't know what my heart wanted.

Then one night I had a dream, a dream more like a vision, a dream so conscious I felt awake while I was dreaming.

I was standing at the end of a narrow room with no furniture. The walls were covered in dark wood paneling and the floors were hardwood. A man walked in a doorway. He had black hair and a curly mustache. He was holding a book and held it up for me to see. I remember trying really hard to "see" the title. I saw a plain book cover with nothing on it. The man's name was Bill. Bill then turned around to leave and before the door closed, I asked, "And who will write this book?" Bill turned to me and said, "You will."

What book? In the beginning, I had no idea. I wanted to look at why I stumbled in the dark for so long, to look at how the messages I received from our culture, combined with my personality traits, created blocks where they should have provided steppingstones. All of my life I had felt alone in my search. I wanted to know if other women experienced anything similar. Were most of us taught to wear masks, to express only conventional sentiments? Had we been taught to hide ourselves as effectively as women who were hidden beneath veils and sequestered behind palace walls? Were other women as isolated as I was?

Though I was uncertain what I was looking for, I began by returning home. I began to interview women from the culture I had grown up in for what I had begun to call my "Gender Project." Later, more than twenty college students assisted me in my interviews. And though women's experiences are varied, many had shared a lack of equilibrium similar to my own. Something was wrong, but I had no name for it. In addition to my interviews, I broadened my reading research. I had to know what taught women to hand over their voice, mind and body to somebody else's agenda.

After three years, through my reading, I discovered other women did have a name for my problem, our problem. They called it patriarchy, the male-dominated cultural rules that have been handed down generation after generation, probably since human beings have evolved. I had one more piece toward solving my puzzle.

But how does patriarchy transmit itself even as cultures rapidly change? Two more pieces were revealed through the voices of the women who came forth to speak to me—conditional love, and what I call "Southern Rules," the traditions of my subculture—the unique instructions that glorify Melanie Hamilton, the woman Scarlett viewed as her archrival, the gracious, beloved ideal of womanhood.

Why am I writing this book?

Sue Monk Kidd says, "If women don't tell our stories and utter our truths in order to chart ways into the sacred feminine experience, who will?"

We are strong and face many hardships and crises. Why can't we figure out what really matters?

—Lee, 41 years old

After four years, I was close to fulfilling the vision of my dream of a book. I had my own experience, plus the voices of women from ages thirty to a centenarian. Our perspective may have been Southern, but our voices, our dilemmas, our struggles are echoed through countless books, countless experiences. In the past, perhaps patriarchy made sense. In order to perpetuate the species—and in our species, the young require long, protracted protection—somebody had to stay behind. If women were out hunting with the men, the lions could sneak in and gobble down the babies. But now women are asked to provide financial support, and it is time to look at the changes that have taken place in the world, and find new messages for women.

Sue Monk Kidd introduced me to the writings of Etty Hillesum, the Dutch woman who died at Auschwitz at age 29, but not before she recorded her own experiences, which still inform us today. "I shall have to solve my own problems," Etty wrote as a young woman. "I always get the feeling that when I solve them for myself, I shall have solved them for a thousand other women. For that very reason I must come to grips with myself."

Many of the woman who were willing to speak out so we could come to grips with ourselves, weren't willing to speak out in ways that might hurt their mothers or grandmothers, women who supported and nurtured them, women who transmitted cultural messages intended to keep their daughters safe. Therefore, I have invented Olivia, a composite for truths that need to be spoken, for no matter who said them, they are the truths that shape and are shaped by our culture. Only by looking at our collective truth can we see what we need to keep and what we need to change. Who is Olivia? Not me, nor any of the women who shared so generously with me. She is the voice of us all, speaking out from behind the mask we still feel compelled to wear.

As I neared the completion of my "book," I had yet another dream, showing me the next step.

I awoke in the middle of the night to a voice saying, "I had a dream. I wanted to be a Queen."

Queen. Not Scarlett, the woman who was willing to fight to better her life and for her man, only to be rejected for her ambitious drive.

Not Melanie, who was as good as she was beautiful, dutiful and demure. Not Cinderella, who, born as princess, sat in the ashes until a man rescued her.

Queen.

"Once upon a time there lived a king who had a daughter…" Thus begins so many fairy tales about women. The king is powerful. The daughter is beautiful. The good and beautiful mother, the late queen, is usually dead. The stepmother, the current queen, is jealous and cruel. The daughter is endangered. Made to sit in the ashes until…, locked in towers until…, poisoned by apples until…, cursed by evil old women to sleep until…the Prince comes to save her. These stories aren't just relegated to old books with pictures of quaint maidens with flowing tresses picking their way through dark forests or Technicolor Disney™ movies. The Prince-saves-girl theme is the gist of every romantic movie and book ever made. It is our story, the story we are enchanted with as little girls. We know when we grow up, our prince will come, proving we are worthy of love, that we are as good as we are beautiful. And if he doesn't, oh disaster, that means we are the homely stepsisters, mean at heart and destined to live lonely, embittered, impoverished lives that no one is interested in. We know what it is to be princess, or not. But those stories don't provide us with a model for being a real Queen who isn't desperately wicked.

We *are* the stories we tell ourselves. A person who has a brain injury may have cognitive and physical handicaps, but will retain her core personality, unless the damage is done to a particular area in the Wernicke's area of the brain, the region where storytelling originates. Without the ability to tell stories, to fabricate her life, she loses the essence of who she is.

Now my dreams were giving a new story to tell myself and to other women who were too old to be princesses, too caring to be wicked, and too vital to be dead. We could be Queens.

Queen. Not Scarlett. Not Melanie. And not Sleeping Beauty who, born as Princess, had to dream for a hundred years until a man woke her with a kiss.

But to invent that story, I had to look back first, to look at the stories that gave the King all the power, and placed the vulnerable, waiting-to-be rescued Princess as the heroine in women's lives. Only then could I begin a story that said, "Once upon a time there lived a powerful Queen…."

When I look at my daughter, Addy, I see in her the woman she will become. She will have questions, yes. She will stumble and think she cannot find her way at times. But I want her to grow up without having to hide her true identity. I want her to grow up without a mask.

So, following my vision of so many years ago, I wrote the book. I wrote it for myself, to "come to grips with myself." I wrote it for the women who, like me, buried their essence even while they worked the best they could for the best of others. I wrote it for our mothers and for our grandmothers. I wrote it for Addy, and for the children to come.

I wrote it because it feels good to be a Queen.

Here's to trading your mask for a tiara. May you wear it every day.

The daughters of your daughters of your daughters are likely to remember you, and most importantly, follow in your tracks.

—Clarrisa Pinkola Estés

CHAPTER ONE

I Had a Dream...
I Wanted to Be A Queen

The drama is this. We came as infants "trailing clouds of glory," arriving from the farthest reaches of the universe, bringing with us appetites well preserved from our mammal inheritance, spontaneities wonderfully preserved from our 150,000 years of tree life, angers well preserved from our 5,000 years of tribal life—in short with our 360-degree radiance—and we offered this gift to our parents. They didn't want it. They wanted a nice girl or a nice boy. That's the first act of the drama.

—Robert Bly

SECOND GRADE. OUR teacher is telling us about a play. Our parents will come to see it. I love plays! The teacher reads this one to us. She explains each part. I know immediately what part is just right for me. I want to be Queen!

"Mama, I'm gonna be Queen!" I say when I get home.

"You are?" Mama smiles. "That's wonderful."

"Don't we have a Queen dress?" My younger sister had been a palace maiden in her play. Her dress could be made into the perfect Queen dress. If I have a Queen dress, Mrs. Ousley will surely know I should be the Queen.

The day of the audition I wait till it's my turn. Afterwards, I march up to Mrs. Ousley's desk. "I should be Queen," I say. "I've been in lots of plays." I tell her about all of them. I don't leave one out. "I can memorize the lines. I memorize good." Then I tell her the most important part. "I've got the best Queen dress."

Mrs. Ousley nods. She tells me to go back to my desk.

I am going to be Queen.

All week at home, I am Queen. I make up lines. I perform for my sister and the dolls. I am Queen. I wear a tiara whenever I can, even to eat and sleep. Yes, I am Queen.

Mrs. Ousley announces the parts on Friday. Each child will have one. We listen for ours. She calls out lots of parts. Finally she gets to mine. "The Queen will be," she says…"Folly Ann."

Folly Ann? My best friend? But she is all wrong for Queen.

I almost don't hear Mrs. Ousley call my name. "Allyn will play the fairy godmother," she says.

I nearly cry when I talk to Mrs. Ousley later. "I thought I was Queen. Folly Ann is too quiet and shy to be Queen."

"That's why Folly Ann needs to be Queen." She says. "You've already got enough self-confidence for all of us."

I cry when I get home to Mama. "I want to be Queen. I want to be Queen."

Mama holds me. She can't help me. I want to be Queen, and they won't let me.

The Wrong Lesson

Mrs. Ousley promised when I was older, I would understand why Folly Ann needed to be Queen instead of me. Now, as an adult, I do understand. But I'm afraid when I was seven I learned a lesson Mrs. Ousley never intended. I learned quiet little girls got noticed. I learned noisy, bossy, confident little girls got second best. Somehow, I figured if you let people know how badly you wanted something, they would give it to someone else. My lesson was, "Ask and you sure won't receive." I learned the way for a girl to get ahead in the world was to squelch her confidence, push away her assertiveness, and manipulate others. I decided if being quiet was what they wanted, then I would try my damnedest to give them quiet. I couldn't be Queen, so I picked up my mask.

Before the Mask

I had a happy childhood and then you face problems later on and you wonder why...you think, "I had a happy childhood, why is this happening?"

—Martha, 58 years old

Very early in my life, I didn't see much difference in being a boy or a girl. I loved Barbies. I had dolls and dress-up clothes, and of course, my very own tiara, but I liked playing with boys, too. I held my own in neighborhood athletics. The boys never outmatched me, and always included me in any rough and tumble play.

Under five, young boys and girls in many families bathed together. Mine was no exception, and one of my bath buddies was a boy cousin about my age. I knew he was a little different, and realized adults were, too. I didn't give it much thought until my mother explained the 'difference' to me when I was four.

At that age I loved wrestling. The little boy from next door and I would wrestle every day in the front yard. Even though we had never heard about the Worldwide Wrestling Foundation, we knew a lot about fighting, no holds barred. We barreled around the yard kicking, grabbing, and rolling. Momma was *not* pleased, and often intervened. More than once she told me I shouldn't kick little boys *down there*, but it was too effective a technique when I was in a tight spot and a boy had no intention of giving me any quarter.

Except for that little "difference," which was to my advantage, I didn't see any big disparity between the boys and me until first grade. One kid insisted we all play army, and was bully enough to get almost everybody to join in. In his little world, boys were soldiers and girls were nurses. Even at the ripe old age of six those rules irritated me, so I never played. It probably was a good thing because the temptation to kick him you-know-where was mighty strong.

Even though gender divisions had begun by first grade, I stayed one of the guys until the boyfriend issue emerged. After that my girl/boy interactions deteriorated into awkwardness and confusion.

Portents and Warnings

Picture me at five-years-old. Towheaded, with black, round eyes that barely open. Happy. If you had come by my house, you would have seen me giggling and bouncy, playing Barbies in the house, or giving "what-for" to the boys in the yard outside. I felt as special as my parents told me I was. That's how I remember me by day; but even at five, dreams terrified me, three reoccurring ones I can describe in detail thirty-five years later: The Worm, Go-Fish, The Hallway.

Night Terrors

"I'm cold," I say. I hug my stuffed koala bear, and pull my comfy blanket tight.

"I'm cold." Shivering, I burrow deeper in the covers. It makes no difference. The night will soon find me.

I grab My Koala Bear and tell her my plan. "I'll keep my eyes open. If my eyes are open, the 'mares can't come."

They find me anyway. Some nights it's all three. Tonight it's only the Worms.

I am placed in a room with other people. The door is locked. The room is sterile and white. I watch. People begin rolling on the floor. They roll and rock, and slowly they turn into worms. I know if they touch me, I

4

will turn into a worm. I stay far away from them, but as each person turns into a worm the space gets smaller. Smaller and smaller and smaller until a worm bumps me. I fall down and begin rolling on the floor with all the others. I am a worm.

"Mama, mama." I am screaming. I can't move. I scream and scream and scream.

"Mama is here." I finally hear her voice. "Allyn. Mama is here." Mama crawls in my bed. I am sweating. My screams taper off into crying, then whimpering. Mama strokes my face. She is still there, holding me, when I fall asleep.

In the Hallway dream, I am in the middle of a narrow hallway, which shrinks while I stay my normal size. I try to reach a far door as the hall squeezes down around me. In Go-Fish, I play a card game with three burly men. Men I did not know. Men like Brutus from *Popeye*. The men have raven black bristly hair, scraggly beards, and tattoos. They drink beer and smoke fat cigars. They snarl and laugh.

The laugh sounds as awful as the snarl, loud and cruel. They will win the *game;* they always do, and take great pleasure while doing it. And when I lose—always I lose—they pick me up, bustle me to the entrance of a long, winding slide. It's dark. I can't see where it goes. They are laughing like they are still winning when they push me. I plunge down the slide into the dark. I am screaming.

Dreams are personal, and can only be accurately interpreted by the dreamer. Most dreams involve symbolism—sometimes symbols we don't consciously understand. When, as an adult, I began my search for the right livelihood, which ultimately became a search for myself, I remembered these early dreams in minute detail, and the symbolism seemed very clear to me. These dreams were the harbingers of a momentous change that, at five, I would soon have to face. Very soon, who I was would no longer match with what I was expected to be. Even at that early age, I could hear the message. The dreams were the messengers.

I don't know who sent the messengers. My parents did everything they knew to provide us with a safe and loving childhood. My father worked hard to make sure we felt no lack, and still found time to let me know how special I was in his eyes. He was proud of us, and we were proud of him. My mother gave us much time to play independently. She also engaged us in activities for enrichment and learning, while making sure we had lots of fun. We painted, crafted, cooked, and played. We sang together. I loved singing.

Our family did not seem to have the conflicts some other families experienced. My parents disciplined us firmly, but they never overstepped. Our family included loving grandmothers, boisterous and interested aunts, uncles and cousins who gathered whenever they could. Mother and Daddy felt a commitment to the greater community. They enjoyed participation in the neighborhood, and church and civic organizations, so our extended family included not only blood relatives, but also, everywhere we went, supportive people who knew us by name. We belonged. We fit.

Still, the messengers came. Dar Williams captures this process in her song When *I Was a Boy*. The adult of the song remembers the exuberant bravery of herself in the Never Never land of childhood. As a child she was fearless, rough and tumble, grass stained. She rode her bike without a shirt, climbed trees, could almost fly. She could do all the things boys could do. The trappings she added to be attractive as a woman seemed like a loss to her, and she tells the man she's with he has won, and she has lost. The man portrayed in the lyrics counters by telling her no, when he was young, he could talk with his mom, love flowers, cry…"when I was a girl."

So we begin this life as children with a difference, which might only be noticed when we're naked together in a tub. And hormones happen, yes, estrogen and testosterone, so we are girls and boys. But society has to teach us how to be the men and women it wants us to be. Unfortunately for women, the same confidence and exuberance that made us good boys are also necessary to make us good queens—the very qualities that make us not so very acceptable princesses. It's no wonder by the time we are good and grown, we also feel bad and lost.

How does society transmit its messages my dreams tried to interpret for me? What are we told, why do we accept it? What did I absorb that made me trade my exuberance in on a bid for approval? When did I bury my tiara in the back of the closet and forget it?

CHAPTER TWO

The Half Unconscious Queen

The social psychology of this century reveals a major lesson: often it is not so much the kind of person a man is as the kind of situation in which he finds himself that determines how he will act.

—Stanley Milgram

STANLEY MILGRAM, AUTHOR of *Obedience to Authority*, conducted one of the most well-known and controversial experiments exploring the power of authority. He originally postulated that a flaw in German psychology caused the general population in Germany to support Hitler, allowing so many ordinary people to help implement the Holocaust. To prove this effect he conducted "obedience experiments" at Yale from 1961 to 1962.

Individuals were recruited for $4.50 an hour to spend time taking part in a fake psychology experiment concerning learning. A "scientist" instructed the individual, who was designated as the "teacher," to read lists of two-word pairs to a "learner," who was supposed to recite them back. Each time the "learner" answered incorrectly, the "teacher" was to administer shocks to a "learner." The shocks were increased in 15-volt increments,

7

ranging from mild to dangerously severe, with the last two settings merely labeled a menacing XXX. The teachers were told to ignore the learner's response or reactions to pain.

There were many factors in the experiment. Yale was prestigious. The scientist was formidable and dressed in sterile white. The role of teacher and learner was supposedly drawn by lots. The learner was friendly and pleasant.

It was all rigged, of course, and such experiments would not be permitted today. The scientist and the learner were actors, albeit good ones. The shocks were bogus.

Milgram was surprised to discover even though "teachers," ordinary people who represented the working, managerial and professional classes, were often tense or worried, none of them, men and the one woman, stopped before reaching 300 volts, and 65 percent used up to 450 volts to punish the learners. Some teachers worried about who was responsible, but, once assured the scientist accepted full responsibility, continued to administer shocks.

Follow-up experiments by Milgram and others replicated the results, though Milgram found "teachers" were less obedient when the instructions were transmitted by telephone rather than in person. Women, who were included in greater numbers in the following experiments, often were more empathetic, nervous and concerned, but they proved to be just as efficient as men in following the instructions.

Milgram's experiments indicated people, even with grave misgivings, are programmed to follow the dictates of authority though the benefits of those dictates are not evident and may even appear harmful.

Who has more authority over a small child than the child's parents? Children soak up the pronouncements their parents deliver, instructions designed to influence the rest of their lives. The instructions parents transmit are received from their parents, who received them from their parents, and thus the basic tenets of a culture are passed from generation to generation. Cultural expectations create the "situation" from which we determine our "actions." Cultural authority rather than "the kind of person" we are determines what we choose to do. These messages, in essence our culture, are often so pervasive it is difficult to isolate particular beliefs in order to examine them to see if they are beneficial or harmful.

Some cultural imperatives are fairly silly and appear to be harmless. Never wear white before Memorial Day or after Labor Day. The only correct dressing for chicken or turkey is cornbread. And it's dressing, not stuffing. For a young woman's engagement photo, she should wear something dark and a single strand of pearls, and her fiancé should *not* appear in the picture. Age before beauty. Don't put your elbows on the table or talk with your mouth full.

These rules have a distinctly Southern flavor. Some of them have fallen out of favor. But I guarantee if you know the rule, you will be aware of it even if you don't follow it. When you quit following it, you might feel uneasy for years, for you've left the familiar path. In times of stress, you might feel guilty for not adhering to a childhood rule, even though you disagreed with it when you were a child, and still disagree with it as an adult.

By first grade we are well on our way to incorporating all three roles from Milgram's obedience experiment: We become the scientist with a prescribed list of instructions, adding more as we become aware of them. We are the learner, constantly testing ourselves against the scientist's infallible list. And we assume the role of teacher, and administer moral shocks to ourselves when we feel we are lacking. The difference is our shocks really do hurt. Even if our messages instruct us to act in a way harmful to our essential nature, we administer the shock—tense, worried, nervous, but still we administer the shock. In such cases we can't win. If we don't accept the "correct" answer, we punish ourselves. If we do give the answer that doesn't require punishment, we betray ourselves. Either way we will exhibit the signs of conflict: sorrow, anger, worry, depression.

When we leave the realm of table manners and appropriate dress, we enter the darker, more confusing area of identity. What does it mean to be a woman in our culture?

Who doesn't know the story of *Sleeping Beauty*, the young Princess who, having been cursed by an aggrieved fairy, pricked her finger on a spindle and fell asleep for one hundred years, until her prince awakened her with a kiss? Why do so many young girls, full of the enthusiastic piracy of Never Land and with enough verve to declare themselves queen, suddenly fall asleep, and even when kissed by a prince, remain sorrowful and lost? Are our cultural messages the spindle we prick ourselves on? Where do those messages come from, and what is the curse that makes us fall asleep to our essential uniqueness?

The King's Unambiguous Wife

Like the sandman from the nursery tale who stole into children's rooms and put them to sleep by sprinkling sleep dust over them, our culture...has helped anesthetize the feminine spirit.

—Sue Monk Kidd

In my studies during my own "lost" years, I came across a term that I had heard before, but meant nothing to me until I was ready to recognize it. At that moment, literally, a light came on and I realized what it meant to live as a woman in a male-dominated culture, a cultural bias that had been in effect for thousands and thousands of years. In Anthropology circles you might hear it labeled as an Andrarchy—rulership by men. Current self-help and feminist writings label it patriarchy.

Gerda Lerner in *The Creation of Patriarchy* states that many people confuse the limited, traditional meaning of patriarchy—a law giving male heads of household absolute legal and economic power over male and female dependents—with a broader definition, but one that still fails to accurately describe reality. Gerda says, for her, patriarchy "implies that men hold power in all the important institutions of society and that women are deprived of access to such power. It does not imply that women are either totally powerless or totally deprived of rights, influence and resources."

Author Michele Barrett says, "Patriarchy referred to a particular form of household organization in which the father dominated other members of an extended kinship network and controlled the economic production of the household."

For my purposes and for lack of a better term, I will also use the term "patriarchy" to make my point. In the purest sense and to make my point, *patriarchy* is defined as a system of social organization in which descent and succession are traced through the male line. To more clearly state the meaning I am intending, *patriarchy* describes our social chain of command—a system that puts men at the top of the hierarchy and women in a secondary position.

Dream Excerpted from My Journal

I was at an arena. I recognized neither place nor players. Men and women comprised the competing teams. At the start of the competition each team disrobed. Women got down on all fours. The men mounted the women as if they were horses. The women ran laps around the track with the men on their backs.

For a long time I thought of myself as an independent woman—one who didn't fit the traditional role played by women. I did what I wanted when I wanted to do it. I never asked my husband's permission for anything. I wasn't "that" kind of woman. I called the shots.

While reading Sue Monk Kidd's *Dance of the Dissident Daughter*, I realized I wasn't seeing clearly—in fact, I did cater to male authority. But the most important revelation was realizing I had not recognized this source of my confusion and pain. I had not known I was testing myself against the rules established by patriarchal thinking, and always punishing myself for choosing the wrong "answer." When Kidd revealed she "behaved in seemingly independent ways, but inside…was still caught in the daughter-hood," I realized she was describing me. Meaning, I always second-guessed myself and constantly criticized my actions and words. I altered myself to play a part—the good, strong girl. Without the ability to rely on myself or to stop the onslaught of self-doubt, I was afraid to move, afraid to ponder, afraid to live. My desire to please shaped all my actions. I was proud of myself for not acting like a woman—whatever I thought that meant. I was pleased that although not a woman's woman, I was also not a tyrannical, angry bitch. I had meshed the soft, demure feminine side with some respectable masculine traits, and what I had created was an *unambiguous* woman shrinking to a patriarchal society.

The idea of the unambiguous woman was first introduced by Deborah Cameron, and further explored by such writers as Carolyn Heilbrun and Sue Monk Kidd. In Heilbrun's interpretation, the unambiguous woman places the needs of others, particularly her husband's, before herself. In *Writing a Woman's Life* she asks, "What does it mean to be unambiguously a woman?" Then she answers, "It means to put a man at the center of one's life and to allow to occur what honors his prime position. One's desires and quests are always secondary." She is the woman who has accepted her secondary status in the patriarchal society. Emily Dickinson in *Love's Baptism* calls such a woman a half unconscious queen. Kidd defines *husband* as "male authority itself, the cultural father or the collective rule of men in general." In my case, it was the collective rule, or rather, the notion of male authority dictated by the culture I had grown up in. The ambiguous woman, on the other hand, feels she has as much an authority in her own life as man has in his. People, including the woman herself, don't know how to react to an ambiguous woman.

There are no cultural precedents for a woman who does not stay within the familiar boundaries.

When I examine the aspects of patriarchy that formed our culture for centuries, refined by the particular culture that indoctrinated me—the South of the United States in the second half of the twentieth century—I am reminded of the story of how mighty circus elephants are trained: shackled as infants, they cannot break their chains. By the time they are adults, chains only strong enough to restrain infants will keep them in captivity, because they no longer believe they can escape. My experiences and those of other women might make some of the more common actions of patriarchy seem harmless and easily dismissed, but remember, these are merely symptoms of an underlying thought process, which formed all the rules of our behavior. We can ignore those rules if we wish, but if we are not conscious of them as rules, we will always feel as though we have given the wrong answer, remember Milgram? Then before we know it, we feel the jolt of mental punishment.

Among the women I interviewed, most of those over the age of sixty-five remembered being made to wear dresses for all activities—even while playing. Many claimed they played "just like the boys, but in a dress." One woman said, "We played domestic games, so the fact that I couldn't wear shorts or pants didn't hinder my play." Women born ten years later grew up allowed to wear shorts, jeans, pants and t-shirts, but for playing only.

Wearing shorts or pants while shopping was construed as ill mannered and provocative. As late as 1968 women could not wear pants to classes at Delta State University. "If it snowed, we had to call the Dean of Women to see if she thought it was cold enough to give women permission to wear slacks," one woman said. "The next year the rules changed."

She also said women couldn't smoke in public, but men could. And men had no dorm curfew, but women did.

Even though dress codes have drastically changed and smoking in public is almost universally prohibited for everyone, fifty years is not that long ago. The mindset that established these particular rules excusing men while applying restrictions to women has *not* disappeared, even if some of the superficial trimmings have changed.

And not all of the trimmings have changed. One subject said, "The television confirmed what I suspected all along. Women were supposed to clean and serve. Men were supposed to have fun."

In my interviews with various women, the question about domestic responsibilities provided dramatic answers concerning a patriarchal informed society. Most of the women interviewed claimed as children they were responsible for household chores, while their brothers did the "farm" work or no chores at all. Many of the women in the over-sixty-age group toiled long hours—to help gather the cotton, work the fields or manage the house. Only in those circumstances, when the family's livelihood depended on it, did the women venture out into the world of men. A native of Arkansas explained, "The girls had to do the inside chores like laundry, cooking and housecleaning. The boys did anything outside the house such as yard work. But, we all worked in the fields—chopping and picking cotton."

A fifty-three-year-old woman said, "We did the inside chores. My brother's job was to take out the trash. He only had to do one job—take out the trash." Another told me, "I was encouraged to spend time in the kitchen, but I really didn't like it. I knew how to clean up really well. I sure didn't care about doing that on a regular basis." A forty-seven-year-old woman explained, "We all had to share in the household chores before we could go outside and play. When my little brother got older, though, he was only required to take out the garbage." A fifty-five-year-old subject said, "I was assigned the cooking and the cleaning. My brothers didn't have to do anything." A woman born in 1928 said, "My chores were inside the house. My brothers had to feed the pigs, cows and horses. I had to wash dishes, help mother in the kitchen and take care of my father and brothers."

"When girls got old enough, they helped put the food out and clean up at big family gatherings," one woman said. "The boys sat around with the men or played. One year we staged a revolt and hauled boys into the kitchen to help wash, but everybody knew it was a game, and it didn't last. In the privacy of our homes, men sometimes helped with dishes, babies, even housework—never in public, though."

Another woman said after about an hour of cleaning the kitchen after the big holiday meal at her in-laws, her young brother-in-law came in for a drink. "At least let us finish this round of dishes," she said. 'At least I didn't ask you to bring it to me,' he told me. The sad part is that he really thought he was being helpful."

As I was growing up whenever groups of people got together for celebrations or fun, it seemed that the men always enjoyed themselves more than the women. Men watched the big game, ate hors d'oeuvres, and drank beer while women cooked, cleaned and served.

As often as possible, I angled ways to escape the kitchen, which meant joining the men in the den as long as I dared. No matter, doing so left me angry and frustrated because being good meant missing out on the fun, but not helping made me feel bad.

A twenty something subject shared another perspective, "I didn't find a place in either world. To me, hanging out with the men wasn't fun, either. Because being a girl, I wasn't as schooled in football lore, politics, or economics. I ended up feeling stupid. I didn't like the stereotypical expectations for me, but I didn't have the tools to cut it with 'the men.' Culturally speaking, girls weren't taught how to talk about these things."

I tried to be different than my mother.

—Jan, 54 years old

We would go to see my aunt and her family in Louisiana. We were horrified. We had chores, but my male cousin would go off and play ball and his sisters would have to cook his meals and clean up his plate afterward. That would make me so mad for them. I felt like it wasn't fair.

—Kathryn, 52 years old

As a child I thought there was one place for men and another for women. Women stayed home with the kids. They were housewives, and were primarily responsible for anything related to household and the children. If a woman worked, it seemed she was a teacher, a nurse, or a secretary, job reserved strictly for women that paid women's salaries. The man, the husband, was the breadwinner. He also had more apparent leisure time, and more fun things to do in it.

To me, men's voices were more powerful. What they had to say was more interesting. Many women seemed to be as frustrated and angry as I felt. According to the way I viewed life, they had put all their eggs in one basket. If this marriage didn't work out, what the hell were they going to do? I envied the men who benefited from the domestic heroics of women, but I was mad at them, too. In my youthful arrogance, I thought I had diagnosed what was wrong with the world around me, and I wanted no part of it.

That's where I feel shortsighted. My parents never said, "Girls can be anything they want to be when they grow up." They never encouraged me. There was always this expectation that you grow up and get married.

—Olivia, 55 years old

Getting married and having children was what was expected. It was not what I would say I wanted. It was expected. That was what life was like growing up in the south.

—Diane, 56 years old

Many women not much older than I could not imagine a destiny other than marriage. I, also, understood women needed to master home management so men and children could thrive. But both of my parents encouraged me to shoot for the stars, and they provided me with many opportunities to ensure I had the skills to do so. By the time I was ready to begin my adult life, the social milieu had drastically changed. By then most women I knew were planning on careers in addition to families, and not necessarily in traditionally women's fields.

On an historical level, we were part of what some social scientists have called the 'sandwich generation,' caught between the traditional families in which we were incubated and the equal-opportunity world into which we hatched, wide-eyed and expectant.

—Susan Maushart

There I was, wide-eyed and expectant, sure the stars were mine, and well aware of what I was *not* going to be. What I failed to consider was the power of authority that had imbued the culture I had grown up in. If there was a man between the stars and me, even if I was right and he was wrong, I was still wrong. Zap. Turn up the voltage. While intellectually I understood men did not rule the world, emotionally I was still trapped in the kingdom of my birth. So deep down, no matter how much I spoke out or postured otherwise, according to my interpretation of my cultural code, if men weren't the authority, who was? Nobody ever acknowledged my authority. Self-confident little girls will never be Queen.

My childhood nightmare of Go-Fish finally made sense. I wanted to have all the fun and sense of a huge presence in the world I thought men had, but believed if I dared join the game, their exaggerated masculinity and overwhelming power ensured I would always lose. I had accepted the chains of my belief as well as any little performing circus elephant.

To succeed meant the foundations that nurtured me, sustained me, and infuriated me had to crumble. And without foundations, no matter what I did, how successful I might seem, I was actually spiraling downward in a free fall with nothing to hold on to.

CHAPTER THREE

Kingdom Rules, Southern Style...
Membership is Non-Negotiable

Rules of the Realm

This pool of belief patterns or 'collective unconscious,' as Carl Jung called it, gains validity as it moves through time, and eventually the concepts that later generations experience as physical reality become rigid and domineering. It's as if billions of people who preceded you have determined what you're going to experience on the earth plane, and that's all there is to it.

—Stuart Wilde

ONARCHY—SINCE MY QUEEN dream, my own particular name for patriarchy—has been the intrinsic power structure since pre-history. It is supported by localized mores: those customs so entrenched they seem to be law to the citizens of the

17

particular realm in which they apply. The nuclear family, the extended family and social groups the nuclear family is allied to, the region, state, country—for all of them, specific rules apply.

Members understand the rules, and most members avoid challenging them. Those members play nice. Even if doubtful, members are more concerned about maintaining order, the status quo, than challenging inappropriate or outdated laws. My realm was the American South in the last half of the twentieth century, where nice girl rules were refined to cinch as tightly as Scarlett O'Hara's corset. Who can forget Scarlett holding onto the bedpost, demanding Prissy tighten the laces until her waist was an incredibly small 17 inches? You can't rebel if you can't breathe.

Shirley Abbot addresses the Kingdom rule structure, specifically the Southern directives in her book *Womenfolk:* "The legacy passed from mother to daughter is everywhere ambivalent and complex, full of unconfessed wishes and unadmitted bequests, woven with demands and admonitions, some of which contradict the rest."

In *Woman Warrior*, Maxine Hong Kingston tells of being Chinese, and raised as a first-generation American. Foreigners were ghosts to her parents, and you didn't tell ghosts your secrets—secrets gave ghosts power over you. Because their American-born children were half-ghosts, the Chinese parents guarded their past, so the half of the child that was a "ghost" couldn't do them harm. Kingston often felt she was clueless, desperately seeking information for why her parents acted in certain ways, so she could place her own life in meaningful context.

We, from our mothers, and they from their mothers, receive the messages: you are loved; you can accomplish great things, but don't want too much; don't follow the crowd, but don't be individual enough to give the neighbors grist for the gossip mill; tell the truth, but lie if necessary; make me proud, but don't get yourself noticed; don't tell family business, and if you do "mess up," don't tell anyone. In fact, they withheld much from their daughters, so we, too, were often half-ghosts in their lives. From generation to generation, the legacy Abbot addresses flowed like an underground river, emerging in our own lives as behaviors we can't quite comprehend. "Be nice," we learned. "Be nice, even if it hurts."

Yes Ma'am. Thank You, Ma'am

Everybody wants their child to have all the perfect manners and do all those things perfectly. And, you want to hear others say, "Oh, what a wonderful child you have."

—Olivia, 65 years old

Southerners are renowned for good manners, and any breach by a child was usually met with immediate and exacting correction—a good swatting by a stripped-down branch was the choice instrument of instruction preferred by my neighbor's housekeeper, and none of us kids was exempt. One woman I interviewed told me, "My Mama would get out a brush or ruler. I was often swatted due to my inability to show the proper respect—such as saying things like "Yes, Sir. No, Ma'am. Thank you!"

Under the good manners edict was the injunction that children should be seen and not heard, though an eighty-two-year-old woman lamented, "Children weren't heard nearly as much in my day." We were probably noisier than children eighty years ago, but when an adult said, "Hush, right this minute," we knew we had gone past acceptable limits. We also knew drawing attention to ourselves was a terrible breach of manners. Attracting attention, even if it was for a positive accomplishment, felt unseemly even in my adult life. Out in the world, when I needed to stand my ground, I not only had to make my point, but push myself to speak up, to be heard. And, I would usually feel guilty after.

Sela Ward described her own experiences with the "good manners" law. "Even children of my generation were made sharply aware of the importance of manners, of their role as a moral compass to guide you through life. From our earliest years we were half-consciously aware of the discipline grown-ups showed around each other and we knew we were expected to follow suit. Our parents, and the parents of our friends and neighbors, lived within well-defined boundaries of behavior. And as we grew older, and began holding our own in social settings like school and church, we came to recognize the practical value of manners. If you knew how to be courteous and considerate, it became apparent, you could enter

19

into any social situation with confidence—and you were much more likely to get what you wanted."

So what is wrong with good manners? Nothing. They are valuable for the civility with which we conduct our lives with one another. Only what so many of us take to heart as children is not the essential purpose of manners, but the emphasis on what other people think. When manners become a law unto themselves, the opinions of others become more important than any opinion you can hold for yourself.

Good manners went a long way toward getting you what you wanted. Good manners ensured you would be invited back to other people's houses. If others consistently invited you to "come back and see us," then your mother could rest assured that her work had been accomplished. I understood early on anything I did, or even thought, which did not meet the approval of the folks around me, was bad. Those "bad" parts I did my best to hide and pushed them far down into the dark.

For me, good manners were about fitting in. It was like Momma went to the store before I was born and got a pattern in every size for a dress—one just like all little girls wore. The pattern was perfect. She carefully cut the pieces and sewed them together, and with much love gave the dress to me to wear. It was a pastel dress with pink flowers and a lace collar, and everybody loved it and told me how sweet I looked in it, but what I always wanted was a velvet dress, purple and gold and black. Turned out everybody thought the dress was perfect. But inside I knew it didn't fit. I was definitely not the person I was being encouraged to become, and I couldn't let anybody know.

I had to remake myself to fit into that dress, those cultural ideas that everybody else seemed to think were the only way to be. Seems like I ended up wearing the pastel dress for most of my life. By the time I allowed myself to wear the dress I always thought I wanted, it didn't fit anymore.

—Olivia, 40 years old

Being Mad Was Bad Manners

Anger. If good home training instructed you to please your momma and daddy, your aunts and uncles, your teachers, your neighbors, and the shop clerks, anger was definitely dangerous. You might have your private temper tantrums with your immediate family, but under no condition was anybody else supposed to see you were angry. Anger meant exposing the part of your being Jung called the shadow self, the parts Olivia hid so she could fit in her pastel dress. Not only did I not know how to express anger, but I also didn't understand the emotion—and I certainly didn't want it directed back at me. It was important for me to be liked by others.

Didn't matter if you were a complete stranger or a long-lost friend. I wanted—No!—needed to be liked. Under the stern dictates of good manners, I never grasped someone could be angry at my behavior and still "like" me. To me, anger meant disgust or disappointment. To be angry with me meant that you didn't like me, approve of me or want me around. I didn't see adults arguing. Mad children were bad, rude children. Whether subtle or not, I understood anger to be a bad emotion—one not to express or share, one that was damaging, hurtful, one that required suppression. I took the lesson to heart and tucked my anger tightly away. I cringed when someone was angry with me. If I didn't "fit" so much I made you angry, I must have been the bad one—the child who had yelled for purple when everyone knew pink was the color for girls.

My momma told me to always smile even if through clenched teeth and to use my smile to cover up all those bad things I said or wanted to say.

—Olivia, 50 years old

Southern women learned to avoid confrontations or heated arguments. We were not allowed to express ourselves with angry voices. My own struggle with this throughout adolescence brought me much pain and suffering. I knew that I was breaking one of the rules when I yelled, but I was so filled with anger and frustration that I couldn't stop myself. Thus, my attempts at voicing my anger were then followed by shame, guilt and regret. When you lose your voice, it's hard to stop the stomping you get

21

from others. Nancy Sinatra's song *These Boots Are Made For Walking* contained powerful lyrics. It was something we all longed to do to those who took advantage, or that we let take advantage of us. But, in the South, we weren't ready or prepared to do what we wanted.

Ms. Abbott described her own experiences: "If the women's movement of the 1970's has passed right over their heads, however, it is not because Southern women are dimwitted or born reactionaries with the code for Total Womanhood strung along every chromosome (as outside observers sometimes like to claim) but because this complicated legacy passed from mother to daughter sternly forbids open confrontations. I have had a while to think about my own mother's legacy—she died twelve years ago, at the age of fifty-four, and although I am not sure I understand, or accept, what she passed on to me, I can't lay it aside, either. It has begun to acquire its own patina."

Many of the women I interviewed also avoided conflict. "Yes, I try to avoid conflict. I feel like I'm walking on eggshells," one woman said. "I always worry that I'm going to offend someone or step on somebody's toes. It's hard for me to realize I can't make everyone happy." A seventy-one-year-old subject said, "My mother told me one time I would walk through hot coals to not have conflict. I want everybody to be happy." A forty-something interviewee provided an example, "The other day, I went to pick up my medications from the drugstore. They automatically refilled all of them. I had decided to only get one, not all. When he handed me the bag, instead of saying I didn't want them all, I just took them.

I do this at restaurants all the time. Like when you get something different than you ordered and you just eat it anyway. I think we're taught it's the polite thing to do and we shouldn't hurt people's feelings." The majority of the women mentioned words like peace, tranquility.

Although, approximately half of the subjects did tend to avoid conflict, they self-reported they would take up for themselves if needed. A forty-something female shared, "Sometimes I avoid conflict because I'm afraid I will hurt others' feelings. Other times, if I'm mad or pushed up into a corner, then I don't care about the conflict I cause." The other half expressed the need to avoid conflict at all costs so as not to hurt others or to rock the boat. For example, a seventy-eight-year-old woman said, "I don't like anybody to be mad at me. I'll take something (verbal assault or finger pointing) before I want anybody to be mad at me."

The message that came across clearly was if you disagreed with someone, there were only two responses. Either you sucked up your anger and smiled through those clenched teeth, or you bit, meaning you threw a hissy fit. There seemed to be no middle ground between pleasing others and pleasing yourself, no safe commons for discussion. And if taking up for yourself made another person unhappy, you had lost, no matter what tactic you chose.

Most of my life I'd run from anger as something that good daughters and gracious ladies did not exhibit. Perhaps the thing most denied to women is anger.

—Sue Monk Kidd

Smiling Through Clenched Teeth

Not only could you never show anger, but you were also not even supposed to dislike other people or their actions. Respect under the Southern Rules meant never dealing openly with people or actions you disliked. Acknowledging that other people or their actions bothered you denoted a lack of respect, and it was inappropriate to treat people without respect. Thus, if you disliked someone, they must never know it.

When treating other people with 'respect' meant you had no means for addressing provocative issues, the stage was set for passive-aggression. How else could you get out your 'bad' feelings about another person, especially if you had to tolerate them no matter what?

Good manners are truly the oil that lubricates social interaction. Those who have the most trouble standing should be seated first. The person most capable of holding open a heavy door should allow others to move through first. Listening to what another person has to say can clear up many difficulties. Allowing someone to exit the elevator before getting on serves a purpose. But when the manners stop being a commonsense method for easing interactions with others, and becomes a code of behavior that stifles differences and suppresses conflicts, we are kept in check. Perhaps we become a little less human, or a little more marionette, or in the eyes of a rough and tumble girl/boy, full of herself and the world, one by one, we turn ourselves from people into worms, trapped, without arms, legs, and tongues to speak, in a locked room, without any power that is uniquely our own.

Smoke and Mirrors

Southern women, certainly, are not too prudish, as a class; nor was my mother a prude. But she had her rule of silence, and she observed it.

—Shirley Abbott

Growing up, good home training instructed us that not only were we supposed to be nice to everyone, but we were taught, "If you can't say something nice, then, by darn, don't say anything at all." A forty-something-year-old woman laughingly claimed, "Can't tell you how many times I was pinched or jabbed in the thigh with a hatpin for messing up that one!" We were also taught not to express true feelings, especially if they were negative. You might never know that a particular individual hated your guts because they wouldn't dare tell you or indicate such. We learned to smile beautifully to cover up our cussing.

We were to be nice, to speak nicely about others, and even not to say aloud things that weren't nice. If you ever did hear someone, a good-mannered adult, mentioning such unmentionables it was always in a whisper.

"Boys don't need to hear all the little details about things," I remember being told about my almost crippling digestive problems. "They don't need to have ugly pictures in their heads about you."

Southerners like my parents tend to embrace a fantasy image of perfection that will admit no flaw, weakness, or shortcoming. For them denial isn't just a coping mechanism; it's a way of life. When I was growing up,

you'd hear ladies pronounce the name of serious diseases under their breath, as if whispering a word like 'cancer' would somehow keep the affliction away. Things deemed unpleasant—menstruation and sexuality, but also grave matters such as unplanned pregnancy, wife beating or alcoholism—were spoken of only rarely. And, if they were, the discussion was so smothered in euphemism and indirection that it made frank discussion next to impossible.

—Sela Ward

My friend, Margaret Staton, told me her family didn't record divorces in their family history. "We just didn't do it. It wasn't considered 'nice.' Margaret said, "My own father was divorced before he married my mother, but I didn't know it until I was in my early forties, and he had been dead for twenty years! My maternal grandfather's sister had been married, had two children (who died at a very young age from illnesses) and divorced; and this is not in the genealogy. She was considered a 'maiden lady,' an old maid."

When we deny the problematic side of life, we rob ourselves of the juiciness of life. We erase our history—just like Margaret's 'maiden' aunt. We become strangers to ourselves, with imaginations as pallid as our white-washed stories. Not only that, anything in our present lives that doesn't match the sanitized standards must be hidden also.

No, we don't want to discuss Aunt Martha's exploits as casual entertainment, but if we can't examine the difficulties in life, how can we learn a better way? Not only that, but problems too difficult or embarrassing to discuss seem to have a way of resurfacing in later generations. As parents we tend to see those same 'dark' tendencies in our children, and react to them in ways that reinforce the very behavior we wish to avoid.

Think of all the energy we waste making ourselves less than we are.

"You must not tell anyone what I am about to tell you," Brave Orchid tells Maxine, her American born daughter. "In China your father had a sister who killed herself. She jumped into the family well. We say that your father has all brothers because it is as if she had never been born." Maxine is reaching puberty, and the tale, Brave Orchid's 'talk-story' is a

25

warning. Brave Orchid's sister-in-law, No Name Woman, conceived a child out of wedlock. When she began to show, the villagers masked themselves, trampled the family's crops, killed the farm animals, opened the dykes, burned the outhouses, broke in the house smashing everything. No Name Woman gave birth in the pigsty, then drowned herself in the village well. In breaking with tradition, she was robbed of everything, even her life, even her name.

But Maxine tells. She tells the story to us all in her exploratory auto-biography, *Woman Warrior*. "Those of us in the first American generations have had to figure out how the invisible world the emigrants built around our childhood fits into solid America."

Sometimes, in our smoke and mirrors culture, we feel if anybody finds out we broke the rules, everything will be destroyed; thus the past often becomes invisible as we try to fit ourselves into the solid world around us. But the past persists, overlaying its reprimands and wounds upon our present. Talking is cathartic; 'talk-story' is a way to synthesize our experience, and the experience of our mothers and grandmothers.

When the fairy curses Sleeping Beauty, the King declares not only all spindles be destroyed within the kingdom, but also that they will never even be discussed. When Sleeping Beauty happens onto the hidden spindle, she doesn't know about the curse, nor does she even know what the spindle is. And if we are looking at metaphors, without the tools to make thread, how has the kingdom supplied new fabric for new clothing? Does Sleeping Beauty, in old tatters, not have a chance?

Our secrets don't protect us. What we hide becomes a curse. What we examine becomes information. Jung's shadow is only frightening until it is brought into the light. Until then we waste much energy making ourselves less than we are. We keep ourselves in tatters in fear of an ancient curse.

We all need to tell stories. Stories frame events. Once we massage life's traumas into a narrative form, they become less destructive.

—Liz Rigbey

Don't Raise Your Voice, Young Lady

One rule that still causes me pain is the one that taught me to disavow my assertiveness and outspokenness. I learned, mostly in school settings over the years, I was too loud and had a tendency to boss and dominate situations—all really bad traits for a 'nice' girl to have. While living in Texas, I played tennis with a wonderful group of ladies. Tennis can be intense—joy over good plays, frustration over bungled ones, and all your brain chemicals are kicking in so you can win. I have vivid images of my dad slinging his racquet when he didn't like the way a ball landed. I knew he was caught up in the excitement of the sport. I understood, because at times with those wonderful women, I would yell or scream in exuberance over some play. Heck, once I even threw down my racquet. Later, jumping in my car, I'd start rehashing those moments, wondering if what I said was questionable.

"I shouldn't have yelled like that. I shouldn't have said that to my partner. Why did I act that way? Stupid. Stupid. Stupid." Good girls should never act that way.

Caroline Knapp interviewed many women for her book, *Appetites: Why Women Want.* One woman was an editor, a highly skilled and talented woman that had been asked to speak to a group of educators. She accepted, and persuaded her audience by presenting her case brilliantly. "But," Knapp reported, "the minute she walked out the door, she was flooded with shame: She'd been way too pushy, too opinionated, she'd alienated the whole group.

She had to call a colleague to ask for reassurance, and it took her days to realize where her reaction had come from: terrible discomfort with her own power, a feeling that some hideous eruption had taken place, the self exposed as domineering, loud, uncontained."

Her shadow side had emerged—the side that was supposed to remain tucked away, quieted and caged. I wrestle with the same issues—loud, opinionated girls are not nice.

And as I thought I learned in the second grade when I could *not* be queen, opinionated girls are denied the good-girl rewards.

I used to know a woman that constantly said, "I'm sorry. I'm sorry. I'm sorry." She said it all the time. Her continual apologizes were unnecessary and annoying. She is an extreme example of the rule of 'lowering your voice.' Every utterance was a risk for her, so she prefaced with an apology.

Claiming voice is terrifying. I have spent years searching for a better way, a more authentic way of living. Finally, I found my voice. Through this book, I am speaking out. The women who talked to me are speaking out. Still, many choose to say the words that need to be said, but feel the need to claim anonymity, because they are afraid their truth will in some way harm those they love. Some choose pseudonyms. Olivia also speaks for them in this book.

My own anxiety level rose as I neared the completion of the book. I began to worry. "Have I said too much? Have I revealed too much? Have I violated the boundaries of people I love?" Though my mother encouraged me in my endeavors, she also grew uneasy. Like me, she has valued her privacy, and has always believed putting the best face forward is a gracious act.

The book. We were telling. Not all would be our best face. What would happen next?

This. I finished the book. Mother has helped at each stage. She has read it, and made suggestions to make it stronger. For Christmas she gave me a tiara ring, with colors that shimmered under the light as a token of her continued support.

Together we will go forward. At times we will run into the old rules as solid as any wall. We will doubt ourselves. But we will share our stories. We will invite my sisters to add theirs, and we will tell them to our children. We will laugh together, sometimes too loudly. We will get on each other's nerves, and we will love. We will help one another reach our goals. And we will be glad.

What Will The Neighbors Think

But I spent so much time worrying about what was okay to say, what might be safe to ask—so much so that I only felt safe expressing myself in the branches of my grandmother's mimosa tree.

—Sela Ward

For me, it was my grandmother's magnolia tree. I arrived on this planet with very thin skin. It mattered to me what others thought. It mattered to the point that I would do anything to make sure that the opinions about me were good, right or appropriate. My Southern culture exacerbated the problem, making it difficult to do or say anything without over analyzing it.

I recall countless times lying in my bed for hours rehashing a conversation. Wondering if what I said was okay. Wondering how the person took what I said? Beating myself up for saying one particular word or for possibly, heaven forbid, hurting another person's feelings. Anguishing over what the other person was thinking about me. "They must think I'm really stupid. What an idiot I am. Why did I say that?" I imagined them worrying or talking bad about me. I simply knew that they were agonizing over every word, just as I was, and I was sure all fingers were pointing at me. The idea that I thought others would be so obsessed with my words speaks volumes as well.

I think back on all the missed opportunities because I worried about what others thought. I didn't want to be a showboat or to behave inappropriately. And, by all means, I didn't want to draw extra attention to my activities or actions. Instead, I would walk away. I would refuse to participate.

I so desperately needed to be liked by people that I often damaged myself in the process. My need to be liked outweighed my regular sensibilities—in college I alienated my future husband while trying to fit in with the girls that *never* liked me. I focused on my weaknesses and inabilities to *say what I really meant*. I regularly slunk away to avoid making a fool of myself or giving others a reason to know I was unworthy.

"What will the neighbors think?" became a constant theme. Ruth Jamison, in Fannie Flag's novel *Fried Green Tomatoes,* lady-like and proper, worried about the opinions of others, about her own reputation—a tarnished reputation being the worst possible calamity in the Southern Realm. For her friend Idgie Threadgoode, the rules Ruth tried to follow scrupulously made a world as tight as the shrinking hallway of my dreams. Idgie bucked the system. Her insistence on flaunting the small-making rules constantly got her into hot water. It was Ruth's job to keep Idgie within society's constricts, but she couldn't bring herself to extinguish Idgie's bright spirit—and Ruth began to find herself living vicariously through her rule-bending friend.

Southerners for the most part, whether male or female, learned to be concerned about the opinions of others. That is what makes us so likeable, personable and friendly. To this day, dismissing the opinions of others is difficult. Writing this book, revealing so many 'secrets,' has stirred up those old currents.

Not too long ago, I had yet another dream. I was back in college, surrounded by a group of girls. The girls were ignoring me. I knew they planned to exclude me by demonstrating how much they disliked me. I couldn't understand why on earth they didn't like me. Why were they doing this to me? Why was the situation so out of control? I cried uncontrollably. I begged the Universe to intervene. I asked for mercy. Nothing happened. Then a voice boomed from the heavens above me. "Allyn, you cannot be liked by everyone. Let it go."

Suddenly, I was at peace with my fears—concerns and pain magically disappeared. I had learned, one more time, knowing what other people thought simply doesn't matter anymore. Actually, it never had.

Still, again, today, I found myself playing those old tapes: "Do they like me? Should I have said that? Oh, I'm being too pushy." Will it ever stop—the sick little need to feel worth from the approval of others—even strangers? Marion Woodman, author of many books on femininity claims we, as individuals, are not being loved as ourselves and therefore we are compelled to hide our worse parts.

She says, "Even in analysis, we will hide our worst faults, and if we begin to sense that we are being loved, even with all our ugliness and darkness, there is an immense fear and resistance, because we feel vulnerable."

Those little voices whispering to me—telling me to stop acting this way and that or else—are voices from the past. "Don't be too pushy, too loud, too dominant." Those are all bad, very bad traits—too masculine, thus, to be avoided. Those aspects represent my shadow side. The dark part of me that, if ever peeks out in the light of day, makes me unlovable.

Right? Isn't that what we think? That if we show all of ourselves, then 'they,' all the others, will run away? Yes, some people may leave, but others will stay. I have to remember the message from my dream. "You can't be liked by everyone." It's the truth—you just can't.

Wayne Dyer said it best: "You'll find no shortage of opinions directed at you. If you allow them to undermine your self-respect, you're seeking the respect of others over your own, then you're abdicating (handing over) yourself."

Something else Dr. Dyer shared in his book *The Power of Intention* that clearly makes the point. "Your reputation is not located in you. It resides in the minds of others." He goes on to tell us that we have no control over the mind of someone else. What they think is what they think. Dr. Dyer explains further, "Leave your reputation for others to debate; it has nothing to do with you."

If the neighbors are discussing you, it probably means they simply don't have enough to do with their time. But in all likelihood, if they are sitting behind their pulled-down shades thinking about you, they are probably wondering what you think of them. Isn't it time we get on with our own lives, doing what we always wanted to do? Then when we meet up, we can tell each other about it.

"Ruth," Idgy says, "you've got to stop worrying about what other people think.

—Fanny Flagg

Patiently Endure

Like so many women I know, I grew up understanding that self-worth and likeability were inextricably linked, that a sizeable portion of my value would come from nourishing others: pleasing, avoiding conflict, concealing my own needs and disappointments.

—Carolyn Knapp

Patience is a virtue, no doubt about it. Without the ability to delay gratification a truly independent adult life cannot be achieved. But what are the messages that induce many women to always put themselves last, and often to feel like last never comes? Is it patience or emotional neediness? In the world prior to the last half of the twentieth century, labor was intensive for most of the world's population. Somebody had to hunt, and somebody had to take care of the children. Doing both was not an efficient way to ensure survival of the species. The hunters had to be ready on a moment's notice to dash off, leaving the family behind, to get out there and bring home the bacon. But once the bacon was home, a different sort of attention was needed to fry it up, feed it to the babies, and make sure those babies were safe through the night.

Patriarchy, or Monarchy—the King's World. The man needed to be 'freer' than the woman, and I am sure women's patience and men's lack of minute-by-minute interest in childrearing is a result of DNA, demands of a labor-intensive culture, and centuries of adaptive rules.

Several of the women I interviewed felt it was a woman's job to sacrifice her needs for the needs of others. One subject that cried during the interview, continued to cry as she addressed this issue, "I sure do. It's hard to explain. If anybody needs anything, I take care of their needs before I take care of my own." Similarly another woman focused entirely on her family, "My kids come first. Whatever they need. If I have to give up or suffer a little, I'd rather do that. Yes. That's what I do." A traditional housewife and mother shared her views, "To be a good wife and mother that's one of the first things you have to learn. You learn a little bit of it when you are first married. Probably your first experience of it is learning that you have to put the needs of your husband before yourself. You learn a whole lot of that from being a mother. Your family will always come first—it just comes with being a mother. I don't know how I do it."

It was as if at some point they had been handed special kind of glasses to view the world, and now even though this world was slightly off-balance, slightly bewildering, they didn't know another way. If this were the way things were supposed to be, and it didn't feel right, then they must be what's wrong...not the world that demanded sacrifice even if sacrifice wasn't necessary or even beneficial. It was just how things are.

But today, the world really has changed. It is now understood that both men and women have the mental capacity for doing the same kind of tasks in the workplace, and machines have made tasks requiring strength gender-equality opportunities. Families are smaller and women don't spend the majority of their years raising their young. The rules have changed, but the messages have not.

I want everybody to be happy and satisfied and I go out of my way to try to please and make everyone comfortable.

—Olivia, 35 years old

A minor form of despair, disguised as a virtue.

—Ambrose Bierce

Many women put the needs of others before themselves, and claim that was simply part of their duties as mothers and wives. "Put the children first," was a motto spoken often. I had a person tell me that her mother always used whatever money they had left to buy the kids new clothes or boots and as a result would ignore her own needs. "But she'd remind you of it regularly. No matter, though, she did it. She needed clothes just as much as we did, but she'd spend it all on us anyway." It's still a female tradition to give up self for others.

Sela Ward speaking about her mother said: "She made a kind of faith out of denying herself, as if even a well-deserved pleasure were a sinful indulgence."

What happens to many a woman is what begins as patience becomes toxic care giving, where everybody's needs but hers are taken into account. And when the burden becomes too heavy, the caregiver finds herself angry, depressed or both.

Even sadder are the women who are *not* struggling—who have forgotten that they have selves worth defending. They have repressed the pain of adolescence, the betrayal of self in order to be pleasing. These women

33

come to therapy with the goal of being even more pleasing to others—to lose weight, save their marriages, or help their children. When I ask them about their own needs, they are confused by the question.

—Mary Pipher

My mother was the caregiver too, but resentful, angry and unhappy much of the time. She didn't pamper herself at all. We had nice clothes, but she usually wore dumpy ones. As a little girl, I loved the rare occasion when she dressed up and went to a party—smiling and laughing.

As a teenager, there was a turning point—my parents lucked into a free one-week trip in the Caribbean on a 60-foot sailboat. My mom went out and bought all kinds of wonderful, new clothes for herself (and started smiling more and being kinder to herself in other ways). When she respected herself more, I had more respect and admiration for her. I see that with my children too. And when I take good care of myself, I'm teaching them how to treat themselves (and others) well...

—Kelly, 36 years old

Patience must be tempered with self-awareness and self-love. The biblical admonishment to love others as you love yourself proves to be true, and reciprocal. If you cannot love yourself, you cannot really love others. You can only give and give and give, and hope they notice, and eventually rage when they do not. But when you take time to patiently nourish yourself, you create the reserves that allow you to nourish others, also.

Olivia shares...

My friend told me jokingly, "I looked at my husband and thought, 'I already have one special needs child—why do I need two?'"

—Olivia, 52 years old

What patient women often want in the end is the same kind of care and attention they lavish on their families. Too often family members don't know how to reciprocate—it simply isn't in the job description. So it's up to the 'caregiver' to show them by taking care of herself. And everybody is happier.

Not Saying No Is What's Hard

Guys seem to feel more comfortable saying "no" and I can't do that. Now, that's generalizing, but women seem to have a harder time saying "no."

—Kathy, 35 years old

No—the pearl in a woman's mouth that would shake the very foundations of the Kingdom. A word that for many of us sounds rude and uncaring and dangerous. Most of us can't get that word out of our mouths. If patience is a virtue, and other people's opinions are more valid than ours, what right do we have to say no? When your job is to take care of people, and their needs come first, saying no can threaten your identity.

Many of the women I interviewed felt taking care of other people's needs was simply part of the duties of a mother and a wife. One woman said, "I think it's learned behavior. I know that my mother did it. It's almost like if you put yourself first, then you feel guilty. There is a lot of guilt in being a woman." Another took the responsibility of others first even further. "It's really dumb. If I have something that someone wants, I might as well give it to them because I can't enjoy it anymore." She said, "It's *not* saying no that's hard."

The inability to say no is driven by our desire for approval from others. Saying no is selfish. If you are selfish, you are guilty. And worse than that, nobody will love you. "I would transport the computer to and from work so that I could work on my writing at home," one interviewee reported. "My husband would end up playing games on it. He didn't understand why I would get so crazy. He always told me that he'd get off of it if I wanted him to. Once I'd get him off, my mind was so agitated, as well as guilt-filled, I couldn't settle back down to work—telling him he couldn't use it or asking him to get off of it felt like an act of violence."

As I entered my teen years, "No" was my mantra. The trouble was I had no middle ground. If I wasn't going to agree with a lady-like compliance, then saying no became an act of rebellion. A selfish act. I truly believed when I said "no," I was bad, a selfish person, and I went out of my way to prove it. I wouldn't give a guest the best seat. I would grab the largest slice of cake—and even, oh horrors—take the very last piece on the tray. I knew that being selfish was almost a criminal act, but saying "no" was even worse. Not giving my time or myself made me a criminal of the heart.

Men are taught that it is okay to be more direct. Women are more concerned about hurting feelings or not wanting people mad at you. Even though I knew how to say no, I didn't know how to deal with the aftermath and found myself often fretting about the reaction of others.

Our inability to say no means we take on countless tasks we don't wish to do, or even need to do. It means we dismiss our own needs as frivolous. Or when we are determined to put ourselves first, we often feel as if we have gone beyond the pale, we see ourselves as outlaws. For whatever reason, the truth is saying no *feels* wrong to us. Too bad. Saying and meaning the word "no" potentially brings us the most peace.

But over time, with enough pressure from those who surrounded you who seemed convinced that their practiced way was more valid than your way (and, therefore, ultimately better), you gradually begin to release your determination to guide your own life.

—Esther Hicks

Little White Lies

Southern girls invariably, at an early age, catch on to the idea that being honest with men is a basic tactical error. You cannot judge a Southern belle by what you see…It takes a keen eye to know what the performance conceals."

—Shirley Abbott

I never lie. I just go around the truth.

—Erin, 13 years old

For some reason, I learned at an early age to say no to others. Quite possibly it had to do with my energy level. I didn't have much, so it was impossible for me to overdo or overextend myself. The times that I did have the courage to say no, I would discover myself explaining in great detail why, and the why was always a lie. Lies got me out of loads of things without being rude. I wanted to avoid hurting feelings, and heaven forbid I make someone mad. And for work related activities, I felt an uncomplicated *no* simply did not suffice. I needed a really good excuse for not attending, and when the reason was, I just did not want to attend, a lie served best. Better to be nice than truthful.

If possible, I didn't lie. Like Erin, I would go around the truth to avoid hurting someone else's feeling. The Catholic Church even has a name for it—'mental reservation.' A mental reservation is telling the truth in a way the other person is totally misdirected, and the Catholic Church says it is all right to do in order not to put the other person in danger, such as if a killer knocks on your door and asks if the intended victim is there and she is, you may say, "She is not at home." She is there, it is not her home, and a murder is foiled. You might even add silently, "She's not at home to you." And I can tell you, when I relied on a mental reservation, I felt as if I was foiling a murder—mine or the other person's, based simply on a difference in priorities.

I am not the only one. Listen to the voices of the women I interviewed, all demonstrating the old adage, "What he doesn't know can't hurt me":

I have several customers who will pay for their products with part cash and then write a check for the balance, so the hubby doesn't see how much they are spending on their hobby. Another one got a credit card that her husband doesn't know about, etc. But me, no…oh no…I've never…well…yes, I have…

—Annette, 42 years old

Mom hid her purchases in the trunk of the car, and we'd be allowed to bring them out only when Dad wasn't home. Then, we were instructed to wear them gradually, definitely not a new item every day for the next week. If he knew we went shopping, we selectively modeled our new purchases…he saw a few key pieces.

—Olivia, 31 years old

I lied about our finances to my husband. I'm the keeper of the books, accounts, bank statements, and checkbook. When asked point blank about money issues, I would flat out lie. He fretted so much about it. It wasn't that I needed to conceal my 'overspending.' It was simply that we didn't make enough to cover our living and I didn't want to be told to 'stop it.'

—Olivia, 40 years old

My mom consistently warned me not to share certain things with my boyfriend that she thought would spoil my image for him. I was confused about what was all right to share and what wasn't. I had a really warped idea about this, and it took me a while to figure out I could share intimate information with a significant other.

—Olivia, 35 years old

Dawn Walker, author of *Daddy's Girl,* has this to add, "All of mine have to do with money (no, I didn't spend that much) or my single days (no, I didn't sleep with anyone on the first date). However, I have found that I hate all mental reservations. Now that I haven't been single for more than a decade, the lies are all about money. After staying home and doing everything besides earning money, I had to make some changes. I will get my first royalty check next month for my book. This is important because my husband, while he loves me, didn't take my writing seriously until I got a phone call from one of Oprah's producers asking about my story. While nothing has yet to come of the phone call, he recognizes the importance of my writing."

Which, after all, is where little white lies originate from—a lack of power, a lack of authority. A friend told me, "My husband and I were having an argument, and he said, 'It's going to be this way, and that's it.' I asked him why he felt he got to make that decision, and he said, 'I make more money than you.' I told him he was a computer whiz, and I was an English major. He was always going to make more money. Did that invalidate my authority forever? 'Yes,' he said.

Not really, we work most things out, but that underlying premise that money talks is still there. And if the truth be known, if I made most of the money, I wouldn't want him dictating how I spent it."

Age, health, shoe size, weight, how much you spent on the shoes—when you don't feel authentic, when you don't have an authentic inner authority, little white lies can seem like life jackets. What you are really doing is going around the truth to get approval from the Other. And every time you do, you invalidate your own authenticity.

Joan Borysenko, in *Guilt is the Teacher, Love is the Lesson* explains, "It is still sometimes easier to pretend things are fine when they are not, to do things I don't want to do because it is hard to say no, to offer myself up as a victim rather than speaking my mind—to give away my power.

But I have learned that the consequences of these forms of self-deceit are disastrous. They make the moment more comfortable and the future much more difficult.

"I began working on telling the truth," a friend told me. "I thought I was a truthful person, but I discovered how much I evaded information I thought might be upsetting to the other person. While I didn't lie, exactly, I put off telling the truth as long as possible. And I began to realize how difficult it was waiting for the other shoe to drop. I realized my tactics were a way of manipulating other people into approving of me, of approving what I wanted to do. Once I became aware of this, I realized I was the one who needed to approve of what I wanted to do. The consequences were much easier to live with than living a life where I didn't count."

And that's what little white lies do—the same thing as whoppers. Each one reinforces the erroneous notion that your life is wrong, that you are wrong. Each time you tell one, you are chunking off a bit of the person you are supposed to be, and tossing it away. If telling the truth is painful, maybe it's time to look at the life you are trying to live, and to know there must be a better way. It's up to you to find it.

Be faithful in small things, because it is in them your strength lies.

—Mother Teresa

The Sky Is Falling

Mothers are held responsible for children's happiness and the social and emotional well being of their families.

—Mary Pipher

As I was growing up, women held responsibility in the domestic realm—cooking, cleaning, clothes, the children, calling the in-laws, holidays, presents given, thank-you notes for the presents received. I took it to heart, and assumed fault for everything that happened in our immediate family. If hubby expressed his opinion about something related to the house, I took personal offense even though his comments were not accusatory. Why? Because I immediately assumed the blame. Yep. It was my fault. I did it. Or rather, I didn't do it. I wasn't doing my job. Slackered. I've gotten better about assuming blame. For years if anybody just made me feel guilty enough, I would change my behavior as asked.

Kelly Kirkendoll Shafer, author of *29 Ways to Make Your Stepfamily Work,* explained her feelings: "One of my children (now 11) is…well… quite intense—intensely happy, intensely sweet. And when he would throw tantrums, he didn't care where we were. The intensity of his tantrum came spewing out! I knew it wasn't my fault, but I still felt judgmental eyes pointed at me. And it would shrink me inside. I finally realized why I felt this way. Somewhere along the line, I absorbed the message, 'A good mother should be able to control her children.' Ha! Whoever said that was certainly not a mother!'"

Add children to the mix and you've got bigger issues. According to Mary Pipher, society decrees your child's actions are a reflection on you.

Right? We become keepers of the blame, and therefore, we are typically accepters of shame and guilt as well.

She further explains, "Guilt is the message we are given. We're not right enough and we need to improve ourselves. Men don't have the same feelings about guilt that we do. Men don't seem to have guilt on the same level and on a day-to-day basis. Women think: "It's my fault. The sky just fell out of the heavens and it's all my fault."

The immediate escalation of any event into a world-class catastrophe is what psychologist Albert Ellis calls *awfulizing*. Its most amazing feature is that little or no objective evidence is required to come to conclusions of unprecedented gloom and doom.

—Joan Borysenko

Not only do we personally take responsibility for everything that happens, but we also make it worse in our own minds—we 'awfulize' it. We spend hours worrying about things that never happened, create fault when none exists, and then wonder what everybody else will think of us.

I handle things. It's what I do. I can handle anything; forgive anybody for his or her mistakes. The very hardest problems for me to get a grip on are the ones in which it's all my fault. I never forgive myself. And my first reaction when things go wrong is it's all my fault.

—Olivia, 55 years old

Show me a woman who doesn't feel guilty, and I'll show you a man.

—Erica Jong

Too Hungry

The messages may be delivered far less directly, or they may be mixed and contradictory, but if you're a woman who came of age in the latter half of the twentieth century, you've no doubt heard them in one form or another: Don't eat too much, don't get too big, don't reach too far, don't climb too high, *don't want too much*. No, no, no.

—Carolyn Knapp

My granddaddy, not educated himself, wanted all his boys to be lawyers and all of them became lawyers—his sons and grandsons. One day he came in to see me and said, "Now Pinkie, you're special and you can't go to law school. But, you can take Miss Pearl's legal secretary job at the courthouse. She's getting old."

—Viola, 83 years old,
Former Navy Wave Commander

In Prill Boyle's book *Defying Gravity*, Linda Bach recalled an interview she experienced while applying for medical school in 1969. "Then these men started asking me whether I planned on getting married and having children—questions that are illegal to ask today.

When I said, 'Yes, after I finish school and am established in a practice,' this man sitting next to me mumbled, 'God I'd hate to be your kids.' He actually said that. I thought to myself, 'This is not going well.'"

Women in the course of history found their identities in being wives and mothers. Because they did not control income, they usually had little voice in how it was spent. If they wanted more control, they had to make choices that essentially cast them out of accepted society.

Control. That's the issue. And may be why so many women have control issues. If our mothers and grandmothers had wanted too much, they might have wanted to be the doctors and lawyers. Wanting too much was scary for everyone.

When I asked for seconds, and my favorite uncle told me, very gently, that ladies don't eat two hamburgers, I received a lesson that underscored myriads of lessons going back to my dethronement in the second grade. Wanting too much wasn't nice.

While women were responsible mommies for both men and children in the care-giving arena, they were secondary citizens in the economic one. For some women, the husband controls what she wears, buys, or whom she sees. "Don't wear that, it's too revealing." Or, "You can't spend time with Ellie. I don't like her." Maybe she bought an unacceptable book or ordered a new pink blouse. In some relationships women have no privacy. Her husband wants to know who she sees, who she e-mails, what she is writing in her diary. I know of relationships in which women religiously meet the mailman.

Wanting too much becomes a source of shame, and a source of addiction, as well. Eating, drinking, shopping all have their source in shameful wanting, and is such a problem for women.

When I first began looking for my own path, and later when I helped people with career counseling, I discovered many women shared a similar problem. Asked what they wanted, they simply didn't know. They had been so busy focusing on other people, wanting something specific for themselves was foreign. When wanting too much wasn't nice, how could they tell what was too much? All wanting was suspect. So to want anything, they had to want it on the sly. Sometimes they pushed wanting so deep, they couldn't remember what it was they did want. So they walk through life uneasy and sometimes depressed, like urchins with their noses pressed to bakery windows. What they have forgotten is they are Queens, with as much right to a stake in the world as everyone else.

CHAPTER FOUR

Conditional Love

Can there be love, which does not make demands on its objects?

—Confucius

My mother loved me dearly—so dearly in fact that she lost herself in the process. She didn't know how to 'let me in' emotionally, but she knew how to give me a good childhood—one where all the pieces fit nicely in a pre-designed puzzle. We danced a dance, she and I. My mother loved me conditionally and I loved her back conditionally.

—Olivia, 40 years old

Dream From My Childhood

Again I am walking down a narrow hallway. I take a step and the hallway shrinks. I step. The hallway shrinks. I step again. The hallway shrinks more. Step, shrink, step, shrink, until I have no room to move. I am trapped at the end of the hall standing before a closed, locked

door. I bang on the door. I bang and bang. "Let me in." I am crying and begging. "Please, let me in."

HIS WAS MY Hallway dream. As with Go Fish and the Worm, I would usually wake up sobbing in my mother's arms. At five, rescued by my mother's love, I could not explain the horror I felt, or what I thought the dream meant.

But, as an adult, I now believe I was aware even then with each step—or passing day—a part of me was shrinking. As I began to experience myself in the context of my culture, I knew in order to be accepted, I had to be less of the person I was born to be. Good girls were rewarded with love; but, even at five, the good-girl rules made too small a world for me to fit. Locked in by cultural expectations, I would remain small, too.

A patriarchal culture stitched more tightly by local customs is problematic, but not the only challenge. Another one is conditional love. Men, women, boys and girls, all at some point come to this closed and locked door. Conditional love is the reward we receive for saying the right thing, acting the right way, being a child of the culture instead of ourselves. Conditional love shapes a person, distorts her view while making the soul small.

I imagine my mother at this door…and her mother and her mother's mother. Why is it so hard to open this door for ourselves and for the children who follow us?

My goal was to get away from home. At the time I didn't think that was a goal. I was looking for what I didn't have at home. And, that was folks that loved me no matter what. And, I found that in my husband's parents. You know, I wanted his life. I married him to get his life.

—Jan, 54 years old

In her book, *Guilt Is The Teacher, Love Is The Lesson*, Joan Borysenko shares: "Because love is such a potent reinforcer of behavior, we quickly learn to experience and express primarily those thoughts, emotions, and behaviors that are rewarded by love. We likewise learn to repress and deny those parts of ourselves that are shamed."

Parents have a duty to teach their child to navigate within the norms of the culture so the child can become a functional participant in that culture when she or he is grown. Yet much of what is taught stems from a parental need to get the child to 'act right'—or, to be socially appropriate in the eyes of others—to conform to cultural rules that may have lost their meaning, and may indeed be constricting and harmful to a fully realized human potential.

Loving parents from all walks of life extend or withhold love in order to teach the child 'correct' behavior. Disciplining with conditional love challenges the child to figure out what works and what doesn't. Responding to overt or subtle clues, a child only feels *loved* when she gets it right.

A child whose parents use withholding love as a disciplinary tool is not only confused, but more than likely never sure when 'love' will be granted. When she perceives love, or worth, depends on gaining approval from another person, she has to concentrate on performing well enough for the approval to appear—or not, depending on the other person's mood or perceptions at that moment. Conditional love, then, leads to the inability to love oneself or others, but instead to crave validating approval. Alice Miller, psychologist and author wrote in her book *For Your Own Good,* "Children experiencing conditional love are often confused, sad and angry."

I wanted to please my parents. I had a sense of wanting to take care of everybody. I felt a lot of pressure to please my mom and my dad.

—Kathy, 35 years old

Children often learn they will be loved only when they do what the parents want them to do. If the child misbehaves, then love is withheld 'for the child's benefit.' The problem with positioning love into two clearly defined areas is that one does not consider a middle ground—you know, the gray area. And parents who do love us unconditionally, within the guise of disciplining and training, use conditional love to mold and shape us.

David Hawkins, author of *Power Vs. Force,* says most people evaluate others and situations on 'positionalities'—good versus bad, innocence versus guilty, deserving versus undeserving. Hawkins says less than five percent of the world population has progressed beyond this dualistic mentality, so it's a safe bet that most of us (that other ninety-five percent) simply do not have the capacity to love differently. We are all moving along the path we are taught. To test yourself, think about the following. Do you still judge others (including yourself)? Of course, you do. So do I.

Return to what David Hawkins said. Basically, it's virtually impossible for us to move past positionalities in our thinking and judgment. So no matter how much we believe or support the need to show unconditional love to our children and ourselves, we very well might be unable to do so completely.

My parents, although unwittingly, used some form of conditional love to teach me. But, so did their parents, grandparents, and great grandparents. A variation of conditional love was the method of choice for all the people I knew—teachers, aunts, uncles, friends. The legacy has been passed down from one generation to the next. With only the best of intentions and *love* as a basis, it was the tool used to shape and form the children. It was the method that had worked in the past and would continue to work in the future. It was the method that reared responsible, productive adults. Ah yes, it worked, but it worked for a price.

Guilt, Shame and All the Other Garbage

What I was feeling, it's clear to me now, was a growing discomfort with the unforgiving rules of the old Southern social order. As a child I had lived within those rules as within a warm blanket, nurtured and protected by the sense of security they offered—but at a price. This culture of honor and chivalry, which defines Southern society and gives it so much of its decency and beauty, has a dark side, and that is shame.

—Sela Ward

Conditional love relies on two required ingredients: guilt and shame. The authority, or teacher, utilizes praise, reward, and love in disciplining the child, or 'learner.' When the child's performance is not up to par, she obligingly accepts *guilt* and *shame*, the 'shocks' to bring her back into line.

Guilt as defined in Webster's dictionary is:

Feelings of culpability especially for imagined offenses or from a sense of inadequacy.

Shame defined:

A painful emotion caused by consciousness of guilt, shortcoming or impropriety.

The key element is that an individual accepts responsibility for imagined offenses or inadequacies in her character or personality and then experiences painful emotions based on feelings of guilt or perceived shortcomings in the eyes of the parent (or authority). And as Stanley Milgram discovered in his experiments, this is just what we are programmed to do.

For me guilt and shame showed themselves in many ways. Looking back, I know without a doubt that I was praised and disciplined, as well as loved, with a guilt-based philosophy. This child-rearing approach was entrenched in my culture and played out by many a Southern family.

Joan Borysenko used perfect language to define the ways unhealthy guilt can interfere with our lives—stop our happiness and prolong our misunderstanding of self: "As long as we're prisoners of guilt, we cannot discover who we are, because the Natural Child is asleep, and our vitality is low. Bound by the chains of counterfeit conditional love that mortgages our souls to other people's opinions and expectations, we are too busy with all the masks, the false personalities, the people-pleasing, and the addiction to perfection to really live each moment as it happens."

I think I probably do wear a mask some. I think over the years I became less vocal.

—Kathy, 35 years old

According to Dr. Hawkins, "the self splits off and becomes the inner enemy, the victimizer/attacker, and the author of guilt, remorse, fear and the relentless self-judge." We cannot relinquish our essential nature. Instead, we allow the parts of ourselves that don't meet with approval, and thus provoke guilt to splinter off. Understanding this process is key, for these separated parts speak to us. Recognizing the voice is a first step while healing the self means integrating all parts—good and bad.

As Joan Borysenko says, "Admitting how we feel, without getting down on ourselves for feeling that way, is how we learn to listen to emotional messages, free ourselves from the past, and start our psychospiritual healing."

Interestingly, not too long after penning this section, I read in *A Course In Miracles,* "If guilt is hell, what is its opposite?" Good question. First, of all, to me guilt is hell. My struggles with guilt were what created hell on earth. Minus guilt, would such a condition as hell on earth exist? Let's return to the question. What is its opposite? What would essentially be the equivalent of heaven? Would it be a life minus guilt? For me, a life without guilt would be quite heavenly, indeed.

Prisoners of Guilt

Our parents, raised in their own environment of conditional love, raised us the same way. We received enough of the needed ingredients— shelter, basic care, love, kindness, support—to mature into healthy adults and to not only survive, but to also thrive in our environments. We have grown up to be sane, reasonable and strong. So what is wrong about letting kids know they are loved when they do what they should, and are not so loved when they don't?

David Hawkins states in his book, *I: Reality and Subjectivity,* "Everyone (except psychopaths) is familiar with the various forms of guilt, such as shame, regret, self-accusation, self-condemnation, low self-esteem, self-hatred and subtle intropunitive twinges of remorse." According to Dr. Hawkins "Guilt can become a self-indulgence. It uses up energy that is better turned into service to one's fellow man. It is necessary to be forgiving to oneself as well as others or else the ego becomes reinforced with self-condemnation."

After guilt comes shame. Hawkins says, "In shame we hang our heads and slink away, wishing we were invisible." Joan Borysenko tells us, "Shame is innate. We don't need to learn how to be ashamed. It is 'factory installed,' like the fight-or-flight response or the relaxation response. Out of touch with our worthiness, we fall prey to the sense of mistaken identity…We see ourselves flawed, as inferior. Self-esteem is dangerously low."

What creates this reaction to the world? What in our world creates this reaction? For me, it was fear. I was terribly afraid. I was afraid of making a mistake. I was afraid of displeasing authority figures. I was afraid of not being liked. I was afraid of my shadow—my bad thoughts or unlady-like impulses, which I made sure remained hidden from others. So many times in my life, when I faced disapproval, I would distance myself from the situation. Thus, losing the opportunity to learn a new way of being, to meet a new friend…my authentic self.

Guilt and the resulting shame have been time-honored teaching tools to train children. Both of them used, with the best of intentions, to manipulate and punish. Now, don't get me wrong. I am not pointing a finger, or saying guilt and shame the way our parents used it, or the way we've used it on our own children, are a terrible form of abuse. They are not. Unfortunately, using these time-honored teaching tools has a price. Their use teaches us to make use of manipulation and guilt on others and on ourselves. Guilt and shame require the recipient to don a mask, to become invisible. If we're all wearing masks, how can we get to know one another, how can we know ourselves? Perhaps that is what heaven on earth is… getting to know each other as we really are.

Conditional love is not devastating. It is, however, crippling. It requires children to don a variety of masks or phantom selves, and to use energy seeking approval when they could be using the "energy…better turned into service" to life itself.

Consider something Ashley Montagu, anthropologist, said: "Love is unconditional, it makes no bargains, it trades with no one for anything. It conveys the feeling, the in-the-bone belief, that you are all for the other, that you are always available to give him your support, to contribute to his development as best you can. Love values the other for what he is, *not* because he is something you want or expect him to be."

All right. So maybe none of us received unconditional love as children. But we are the grown-ups now. We don't have to keep ourselves in line with shame and guilt. We don't have to slip on masks, and banish essential parts of our nature, our very energy, to silence and darkness. We don't have to use the rest of our energy performing for the approval of others. The time has come for us to see if we are making bargains, to be aware if we are trading our value so we can feel we deserve a place in the world.

Unconditional love is what we receive when we accept ourselves, support ourselves, and contribute to our own development as best we can. And when we do, we will also know how to love our children and our parents for what they are—not what we expect them to be. Then we will discover that door at the end of the cramped hall of cultural expectations has never been locked, and a spacious palace is ours on the other side.

CHAPTER FIVE

The Princess Pricks Her Finger

Dream Excerpted from My Journal

I was shopping with my friends. I ventured over to the shoe depart-ment and started looking at the new styles. The shoes were hideous. The soles were made out of rubber and looked like a tire. I said, "I can't buy these ugly things!" As I walked away, I thought, "I'll probably buy a pair next year because that will be what everyone is wearing. If every-one else is wearing them then so can I."

ONCE IN MY pre-teen years, I awoke from a nap into a foggy world. I realized I couldn't touch anything or anybody or let them touch me, or would turn into those nasty, brown, peopled-sized worms I used to dream about. A babysitter was home with my sister and me. The house became a maze where everything was dangerous. I was sweating as I picked my way through it. When my sister tried to approach me, I began screaming. "Don't touch me! I can't be touched." I mumbled and cried and raved while avoiding walls and furniture, trying to keep far away from my sister and the sitter so I wouldn't be turned into a horrible, gross, worm person.

52

My Dad came running through the front door, headed straight for me. I knew what was about to happen. "No! Don't touch me," I was screaming. "Don't touch me. I can't be touched." Daddy, ignoring my pleas, scooped me up.

I writhed in his arms. Nothing happened. Finally I relaxed.

My mother felt my forehead. She sounded almost gleeful when she announced I had a very high fever.

I had only been hallucinating. I wasn't crazy.

Not yet.

But a crazy was on the way my parents couldn't save me from. Soon I would be a teenager.

At the age of five, I never found an enemy. I loved riding my bike and playing in the fort. I liked both boys and girls, and they liked me. I liked dolls, too, and loved playing with them in my room. Recalling those years, I don't remember being troubled or in trouble, except for the nightmares that began when I was five. Otherwise, I was having too much fun for trouble to catch up with me.

I was a rambunctious little girl with big dreams. When my Aunt Kay took off to New York to become an opera singer, I dreamed about following in her footsteps. I spent many summers watching her perform, and I sang and performed too, creating and acting in plays for family, friends, dolls—anybody who would sit still long enough to indulge me. I recruited my sister and my cousins to put on plays with me.

Beginning school didn't change a lot for me. I loved kickball best— the power behind the kick, the thrill of running—and I excelled in sandlot sports and did well academically. In the 2nd and 3rd grades, I discovered a new aspect to boys—they could be boyfriends instead of friends that just happened to be boys. After that I usually had one boyfriend, but still had lots of boyfriends. Because my growth outpaced theirs, I hung on to my athletic dominance. I was faster than most of my classmates, and usually picked first or second for recess games of kickball and baseball. By eight I was also playing tennis.

I was Daddy's little girl. I was exuberant in my affection with my parents; full of hugs and kisses, happy to get them in return. Nothing prepared us for the conflict and turmoil that would emerge in my teen years.

There Arose a Strong Wind

Most girls recover from adolescence. It's not a fatal disease, but an acute condition that disappears with time. While it's happening… nobody looks strong. From the vantage point of high school, strong girls can tell their stories, but in junior high, they have no perspective. It's impossible to have much perspective in a hurricane.

—Mary Pipher

While I was experiencing my life, it never seemed like me. Surely there was something else I was meant to do. Those 18 years of my life was somebody else. I was discontent. It was like someone else was in control of my body.

—Diane, 56 years old

At age twelve, I started paying way too much attention to boys. Boys liked me and I liked them back. One of my first *real* boyfriends had tremendous influence over how I perceived myself—particularly my looks. He'd say, "Don't smile with your mouth closed, you look funny." Of course, I listened. Not smiling as ordered took practice, but eventually and before he broke up with me, I got it. Later, he confided he hated my neck—too short for his liking.

By thirteen, I began spending more time with friends, and my mother recognized I needed to express my independence. Of course I wanted some distance from parental influences, but that meant I was becoming dependent on what my friends thought—and, at least one of my friends thought I dressed like a kid.

"You just don't wear Converses with dress pants," she finally told me. Until that point I wore tennis shoes with *everything* so I would be ready for whatever game happened at recess or after school. My friend's information had the ring of Law, and I realized not only were my shoes not right, but I also wasn't right. Time for some changes, and those changes meant I had to leave the world of boys-who-were-friends and spontaneous sports.

By 9th grade the new game consumed me. I was moving into the world of where boys and girls were different species, and girls were different from the children they had been.

Always a great strategist, it didn't take me long to figure out the rules, all with one intent—fit in. To be what my friends thought I should be. To never be, perish the thought, different. I didn't even have to make a conscious choice about whether to play or not. I already knew to be loved and accepted I *had* to follow the rules. So I looked and listened, and with each new tidbit of information, I deleted some aspect of myself that was as wrong as my shoes. I picked up my mask. I left behind the little girl who knew what she wanted, and became somebody I didn't know. If you had asked me what was happening to me, I couldn't have told you. I could barely comprehend the turmoil seething in me, or the shame when all of my choices seem destined to fail someone—my parents, or my friends, or the person I had been up until then.

At age fourteen I had essentially fallen asleep, like the sleeping princess Briar Rose in Grimm's fairy tale. I had become the Princess seeking rescue and all the while trying with every piece of myself to go away—slip away in a deep, deep sleep. Once Briar Rose pricked her finger and the spell was cast on everyone within the castle, outside a great barricade of thorns sprang up, keeping all rescuers away. For me life was filled with thorns. To feel was painful. To love was painful. To need something from others was painful.

To be was painful.

And I had no idea who I was in this nightmare. Even my body was changing. I wasn't cute and little anymore. I thought I was fat and ugly. I was always on a diet and subsisted off of tuna salad and a Diet Rite™ as much as possible. My old allies, boys who were friends, noticed. Once at a basketball game, a group of them decided I reminded them of a dog. Every time I stood up or moved around, they howled, barked and laughed. Four of those guys had been my boyfriend at one time or the other as we practiced for the changes that were coming, and all of them had been playmates in our rowdy playground sports. No more. Now we belonged to different countries, and I felt my ugly body had betrayed me as much as they had. They had become the enemy, but not as much as I had become an enemy to myself.

Rosalind Wiseman in *Queen Bees and Wannabes* reminds us of trouble in adolescences doesn't only affect the daughter. "Mothers and daughters seem to have the hardest time with each other…Fathers also have struggles with the child who just moments ago was 'Daddy's Little Girl.'"

From my limited perspective, it was Dad who changed, or so I thought. What choice did he have? They hadn't provided instructions for what to do when the 'apple of his eye' became a raging, out-of-control adolescent. He became my primary target at home. How many times did I run for the sanctuary of my room, yelling, "I hate you, I hate you?" In my mind's eye, I slammed door after door after door because we weren't allowed to slam doors in our house. I yelled. I screamed. When I wasn't screaming, I pouted. Sulked, and used the silent treatment. I'm not sure why. It felt like I had no control over my rages and their outbreaks, so I was also filled with guilt and shame. I cried a lot, especially at night in my quiet, dark cave.

Even my sister and I were constantly at odds. She was only 11 months younger than I, but she did not share my tortured experience. The problem was with me. I thought of suicide, though not actually to the point of doing something about it. Again, in my mind's eye, I remember visualizing a deep, dark hole and praying I could just slip into it. Disappear. I was in excruciating pain and wondering what in the world had happened.

It was around my 8th grade year, the year I was barked at, a boy asked me to be his girlfriend, but only if I wouldn't tell anybody. He was to die for. What was there to say besides "yes?" Later, I dated a string of the *wrong* boys—you know, the ones my parents would rather I not date.

I started smoking cigarettes that year, and sneaking beer. Some friends in my circle introduced me to pot. I was breaking the rules and couldn't stop myself. I was also ashamed, and didn't like the person who was doing all of the things I knew shouldn't be done. I was *bad*.

It only took my parents six months to discover my secret. They transferred me to another school in the middle of the year. In a way I was relieved. Through 7th grade, school had been pretty much a fun and safe place, but the middle school seemed dangerous. Many of my old girlfriends had gone to the school my parents were now sending me to, and I looked forward to being with them again.

While my parents' attempts to stop my marijuana smoking at the time worked, the new school experience still caused me pain. By 9th grade, I started experiencing spastic colon, or what now would be diagnosed as Irritable Bowel Syndrome, so intensely that a doctor gave me permission to come home to eat lunch, supposedly to reduce my stress level when eating a meal.

My stomach hurt constantly. That old cliché, tied in knots, was exactly what it felt like. I developed severe bouts of constipation, which led to laxatives.

Laxatives provided relief with a wonderful side effect—weight loss. For years, I would use laxatives to control my weight and what I thought of as my voracious appetite. During the wanting-I-knew-not-what teen years, I was always hungry. Something was definitely wrong with me. Something had happened to the happy little girl sure of herself and of the world, almost as if a wicked crone had cast an evil spell on my life.

Girls know that they are losing themselves.

—Mary Pipher

Alone in the Woods

Mary Pipher's exploration of the tumult of the adolescence of girls describes well my own journey through a treacherous phase. "Girls are inarticulate when it comes to describing the experience. Language doesn't fit their experiences."

During that time I was at a complete lost for words. I didn't know what was happening and didn't know how to express it. I felt alone. Lost. Directionless. There was a not a soul that I could talk to about my strange new feelings. Not family. Not friends. When I tried, it came out all garbled. Messy. Stupid. Nonsensical. I worried about whether I could return to my former self, knowing that the former self wasn't really the answer either. But the new self, the one that seemed contained, but also so out of control was surely not the person I was destined to be. Filled with so many conflicting emotions, I sought out independence, but still needed my parents. I contained or suppressed my emotions, but in 'out-of-control' moments would rage. Those rages were followed by intense feelings of shame and guilt.

I secretly wondered what was wrong with me. I hated life. Hated the way I felt. Hated the way I looked. One day, I was up and the next I was down. I wanted to get off this roller coaster.

Pipher explains, "Parents know that something is happening to their daughters. Calm, considerate girls grow moody, demanding and distant. Girls who loved to talk are sullen and secretive. Girls who liked to hug now bristle when touched. Mothers complain that they can do nothing right in the eyes of their daughters and involved fathers bemoan their sudden banishment from their daughters' lives. Their daughters are entering a new land, a dangerous place. Parents can scarcely comprehend. Just when daughters need a home base they cut themselves lose without radio communication."

Lost, turning from their parents, filled with guilt and shame, girls try to build self-worth and self–esteem from external sources—boys, girl-friends, media. Pipher uses Shakespeare's Ophelia to explain the process. "In the story of Ophelia from Shakespeare's *Hamlet*, Ophelia, as a girl, she is happy and free. With adolescence she loses herself. She lives only for Hamlet's approval and has no inner direction. Rather she struggles to meet the approval of Hamlet and her father. Her value is determined utterly by their approval." She further stated her point by sharing thoughts of a client, "I'm a perfectly good carrot that everyone is trying to turn into a rose. As a carrot I have good color and a nice leafy top. When I turn into a rose, I turn brown and wither."

At this age kids take many risks in order to prove to their friends they are really roses, and not cartoon carrots…sex and drugs take their toll, both physically and psychologically.

The Breaking of Dawn

Thankfully, for most of us, the turbulence of adolescence is short lived. According to research, most girls do actually survive the process of maturing. The seemingly impossible challenges of adolescence tend to tone down and wane as girls enter the eleventh and twelfth grades.

It took me about three years to muddle through. During those dark years, I even made a speedy trip to a psychiatrist. Without answers, it seemed the safest place to send me.

After a 10-minute visit, the cold and unemotional man labeled the affliction depression and handed me a prescription for an antidepressant. Violently sick for three straight days, I flushed the pills down the toilet vowing never to need drugs again. With depression no longer an option, I substituted suppression instead.

By the middle of my tenth-grade year, I began to see light seeping in, but it was almost the end of my junior year in high school before I awakened to the new self—a self that contained some of the falseness remaining from the adolescent years, but that also took back some of the former self of childhood. In the eleventh grade, *I* emerged carrying many of the good parts of myself while still retaining my need to seek approval from external sources.

I still suffered from acne, spastic colon and anger, but I masked it with goodness, happiness and love. I returned to enjoying life for the most part, though I knew my real happiness lay in the future.

In a sense, Becca is invisible. Her teachers don't see her as someone in need of counseling or special help, because, although her grades have dropped, she is never combustible: she never, for instance, yells in class, pounds desks, fights with other children, conspicuously challenges authority. Becca's is a passive resistance—a typically feminine resistance. By opting out rather than acting out, Becca still conforms to the image of the ideal female student—quiet, compliant, obedient; as such she is easily overlooked, or seen as 'making choices' rather than expressing psychological distress.

—Peggy Orenstein

Why is it so hard to feel comfortable in your own skin? Why?

—Olivia, 15 years old

Many of us face our young adulthood carrying a burden—the hidden parts of us we deemed unacceptable, the part of our consciousness Jung called the shadow. We felt these parts threatened our acceptance, and thus our survival, and are too horrendous for us to even look at. Instead, though we will be competent and self-reliant adults in many ways, we enter the next phase of life still seeking approval and validation from sources outside ourselves.

The American culture's unspoken dictate to young girls approaching adolescence is that they *must* separate from their parents. And on cue, like Sleeping Beauty, we fall asleep to our authentic self. Our loss of identity and familiar support is often so frightening we act out our nightmares. Surely balance returns, and we appear to wake up. What we don't know is we have left some of the most original parts of ourselves in a deep sleep. Thinking we are awake; we act out the fairy tale. Our prince comes in the form of careers and families. We belong in the kingdom once more. We move forward, vaguely disturbed because we can't make all the pieces of the external world quite fit our fairy tale. What we sometimes take years to discover, what we are missing are those parts of ourselves, still sleeping.

Because there are so many individual differences, even sisters come out of the same experience in different ways, one more affected than the other—therefore, we must look at a question posed by Mary Pipher in *Reviving Ophelia*. "The important question is under what conditions do most young women flower and grow?" That is the question we want to ask for our daughters.

Within us all is the power to shape and alter our culture and it is important that we do that while keeping in mind the desired result—finding the conditions under which most women flower and grow while providing the tools to become powerful, loving and spirited women.

The scariest part about entering adolescence was that I thought this was how I was going to be for the rest of my life. I didn't believe that I would get through that period. I couldn't picture who Allyn was going to be once she transitioned to the other side.

As with all transformations, the light eventually appeared. As this sleeping phase ended, I started to wake up. I realized that my boyfriend wasn't whom I needed or wanted. I realized I was tired of sulking, crying and hiding. I realized that it was time to live and be the self that I knew before. Emerging from the fog, I returned to what I knew, reclaimed my extraverted ways and again turned my focus outward. Although I had arrived in a better place, my journey was just beginning. There was a long winding road in front of me with many twists and turns. The new person I unveiled, or returned to, was a person weighted down by many layers and unanswered expectations. It was as I peered out of adolescence and turned toward womanhood that I crowned myself a half-unconscious Queen.

A wannabe Queen who had so much more to learn and live before the tiara could be found, yanked out of the closet and proudly displayed for all to see.

If I could talk to myself on the verge of entering adolescence, I would say, "It's going to be alright. You will survive." I would teach that long ago 'Me' how to articulate her feelings. I would ask her to examine the parts of herself she found unacceptable rather than repressing them. I can't begin to imagine a life without the struggles of spastic colon or acne—the experiences of my youth that scarred me deeply.

Life, of course, has to be lived. Lessons have to be experienced to be learned. But, what if I knew, from the onset, that it was going to be tough, but I had the skills to handle it better? *What if?* What if our culture changed its induction to that time in the lives of its girls and created a safe, nurturing place to experience the first *Change*—the transformation to adulthood.

But before we can keep our daughters from falling asleep, we must look within for those parts of ourselves the prince failed to awaken. We must welcome ourselves as the powerful women we want our daughters to be. To be Queen, we must claim our whole selves. And our daughters will hear us, and learn.

CHAPTER SIX

Life with the Prince

Please don't ask me what the score is; I'm not even sure what the game is.

—Ashleigh Brilliant

Going for the Prize

If you are good enough, right enough, then you will get the prize. That's what I was taught.

—Donna, 55 years old

WHEN I LEFT home for college, I thought being Greek was the prize. I got a bid from what my peers considered to be one of the best sororities on campus. Success meant *really* fitting in. I thought I had made it, the place where I was more than all right, and the world had confirmed it. I had survived early adolescence, that time of not knowing who I was or what was happening to me. Only I didn't realize by what skill I had survived—that I had donned the mask, the one that elicited approval from others. And I had muted my own voice, the one that was unique and different. Unfortunately I soon felt the way I did when I was six, and the first-grade bully took over the game and dictated the roles for the rest of us. Only now there was no me—no bossy, bodacious little Queen who just says "NO!"

I kept playing the game. I didn't know another one to look for. Finally, after trying *really* hard, I shut down. I had sworn off depression, so I didn't allow myself to feel sad.

Instead, I didn't say much, nor did I share myself with others. And to compound my alienation, when my first roommate moved back to Memphis, I asked someone completely incompatible to take her place. Turns out, neither she nor her friends liked me.

If I had been more aware, I would have realized my problems with these young women stemmed from their actions and innate abilities to be unkind. Maybe, I would have understood my own perceptions of myself caused at least half the problem, which might have resulted in distancing myself from them, or speaking out and letting them distance themselves from me. If I had liked myself, I might not have even noticed if these people didn't. Instead, I thought I had to please everyone, even people who were mean to me.

My future husband was on hand to offer me comfort, or I probably would not have survived. I felt like Cinderella among the stepsisters, spending my alone time sitting in the hearth, with no voice to claim what was rightfully mine. Luckily, my roommate had a date at the altar, and her replacement was wonderful. I could then go about the business of courting with my future husband and obtaining the degree I had come for.

An outsider looking at my college years would have deemed me successful. I worked hard to prepare for my future. I found a mutually loving relationship that led to a long-term and very satisfying relationship for over three decades. In fact, the four months I prepared for my wedding, I felt I had pulled out my tiara, and been rightfully crowned Queen. But the one lesson I did not learn at college was one that it would take me years to comprehend. When I reached a place where I felt I should have 'made it,' but was instead uneasy, and often miserable, what was missing was some essential part of myself.

I am not the only one who lacked a sense of personal authority, a lack of an authentic voice. Many of the women I interviewed spoke about their own misgivings. While seventy percent claimed that they revealed their real selves to others, the majority of this group also felt it necessary to hide some aspect of their personalities. One seventy-something woman shared, "I don't have a whole lot of confidence. So, I try to hide that. I also hide my anger." An over fifty something subject moved to tears explained, "I don't let others know how much you can get hurt."

Other subjects said things like, "I hide my temper;" "I hid that I get my feelings hurt easily;" or "I hide my lack of self-esteem." An eighty-year-old female laughing said, "Sometimes I get these little nasty thoughts. But, I ask God to take them away from me!" Yet another subject explained, "When growing up I had to be somebody different than I was. It was like saying, 'Okay, who do you want me to be?' Whatever society expected me to be. I had these feelings if I wasn't that, then I was bad."

Many of the women I talked to felt silenced not by peer groups, but by the lack of role models, the lack of choices available to them.

Women younger than sixty-five related few differences in how they were treated in high school. A seventy-one-year-old lamented, "Up until high school we took the same courses. Then, the girls took home economics, shorthand, typing and business math. But, we didn't take advanced math or science courses. We typically thought those were courses for males."

For the most part, the women born after 1940 reportedly took the same curriculum as their male counterparts, the only exception being home economics and shop. Women learned to be better homemakers while men practiced fixing cars and doing minor carpentry work. This division of non-academic subjects was a not-so-subtle reminder of where these young people were headed after school.

Interestingly, however, many of the women no matter the age, mentioned teachers had higher expectations of their abilities and performance than of their male counterparts.

One woman had an interesting perspective on extracurricular activities. "The guy that I dated…when he was student body president, he had a lot of girls doing the work." That was prophetic for one fifty-five-year-old woman who said, "I've had two bosses come right out and say they preferred women to do the work. The first rain a nail-gun business. He told me, 'A lot of folks don't think women should be carpenters. But I hire them for finish-work crews. They are neater, pick up after themselves, don't come in hung-over from the night before, work harder, won't quit on you because they have babies to feed. Besides this is the best paying job they've ever had. And you don't have to pay them near as much.'"

Twenty years later, her boss at a mental health clinic told her, to her face, "I'd rather supervise women. They work harder, and follow orders without giving you a hard time about it. Women don't question my authority."

This woman's supervisors obviously benefited from the Monarchy's rules for molding young women.

The Princess Takes a Beau

Is this all there is?

—Olivia, 30 years old

For many women, the prize that was going to save them was a man and the family that would follow. But, for the women I interviewed, even the process of finding the prince underlined cultural differences for genders.

To paraphrase Oscar Wilde, boys cannot become mothers; that's their tragedy. Girls can; that's theirs.

—Susan Maushart

Parents of females, well aware that their daughters could easily become mothers, treated their daughters differently when it came to dating. No matter the age, women abided by stricter rules. The males reportedly lived by the motto, "Boys will be boys," and usually had minimal or no restrictions. A subject growing up in a small Delta town reported, "In Greenwood, the girls would all be taken home by curfew and then the boys would go back out." One subject during the interview yelled to her father in the next room, "Are you listening to this, Daddy?" Her father had been

65

stricter on the girls. "I was really shocked to see that my brother did not have to have the rules we did. He didn't have to report in. My parents told me the world was safer for boys than it was for girls. Only thing was, he was younger than my sister and me, and we knew we had better sense than him. He was the one who needed taking care of."

A thirty-nine-year-old subject shared, "I got married when I was 21 years old. The night before I got married my curfew was still 10:30 p.m. The first date I ever had; Daddy met him at the door with a shotgun. I was also restricted to going out one night a weekend.

My male cousins could stay out as late as they pleased and also got to go out three nights." One of the subjects in her fifties shared a similar experience, "Two days after graduating from high school I got married. This is the strange thing. My dad was still so strict on me. Even though I was getting married two days later, I wasn't allowed to go to my graduation party. Makes no sense. Two days later, I got married and left home for good."

A forty-year-old female explained, "Oh gosh, my brother was pretty much allowed to do whatever he wanted, but we girls were not. It was really hard for us. We had to go through a big deal. Who is it? Who are his parents? Up until I was seventeen, I could only go out on Sunday afternoon. It was never a night-time date."

A fifty-five-year-old subject said, "I wasn't allowed to date until I was sixteen years old. There was no single dating. We had to go with other people. My brothers were allowed to go as they pleased. They didn't have a set time to be in or rules, like the girls did."

Five of the women interviewed claimed they were never allowed to date while in school. Ranging in age from 47 to 82, the women provided different reasons for the restriction. One woman shared, "The boyfriends had to come to the house and stay at the house. There was no dating."

Going to the Chapel, and I'm Gonna Get Married

The popular Beach Boys song, *Chapel of Love,* has been the theme song of many a Mississippi Delta Miss. One fifty-something female said, "My mother begged me to explore. She told me, 'Of course we love Johnny, but I would have wanted so much more for you. I remember the day I told Mama and Daddy that Johnny, and I were getting married. Mama looked at me and said again, 'I would have wanted so much more for you.'"

Another sixty-something female told me, "My goal was to get married. The trend at the time was to marry young. I was 21 and that was the norm. My husband's sister was 26 and we thought she was an old maid."

With the women I talked to, not just dating practices, but often career choices appeared to be limited. Even as late as the mid-80's, women in colleges sprinkled all over the South talked about pursuing the "Mrs." degree.

Particularly those over fifty years of age felt their options were restricted. Some never desired to work outside the home, but attended college to be well rounded and educated before marrying and settling down.

The same subject continued, "I think most of the girls that I went to high school with saw very limited possibilities. They wanted to get married, number one, and many talked about being a secretary. Not many of my high school friends even attended college.

Without a Dream in My Heart

It's very sad. In dreams it's the little soul bird—"I only wanted to sing my song." And never sang it. Most people don't even know there was a song to sing. They just don't know.

—Marion Woodman

We had lots of encouragement to excel. It was, however, along very traditional roles.

—Olivia, 35 years old

A fifty-something female expressed her confusion over possible careers. Only now, thirty-seven years after graduating from college is she pursuing her passion. "I wanted to write. That's all I wanted to do," she shared. The writer then told a 'defining' moment story. "During college, a war correspondent visited the campus," she said. "My boyfriend and I attended. I was in awe. Following his speech he had a question-and-answer session. I decided to ask a question. Of course, it's been so long ago, that I don't remember what I asked. But, what I do remember is that my boyfriend turned around and hit me as if to say, 'shut up' and 'don't ask stupid questions.' After the speech, we visited with the speaker and he said to me, 'How pretty you are.' Even though it was a compliment and I liked that he thought that way, I actually took it to mean that I didn't have a whole lot of sense. I figured I was really dumb. I just retreated."

A younger woman in her early forties shared, "I always wanted to be a veterinarian, but I didn't know any women doing that. At school we'd have career day. The teachers would separate the boys from the girls. Women talked to us about being nurses, teachers…things like that. A veterinarian came and talked to the boys, but I couldn't talk to him."

A seventy-year-old female answered, "Girls had about three things they wanted to do. One was to get married. One was to be a teacher or nurse. Marriage was what I wanted to do first. My second option was to be a secretary. Back then girls didn't do much. It was an exception if they did something outside the expectations. The guys were the lawyers, doctors and, you know, businessmen."

A fifty-five-year-old subject explained, "The doors weren't open for a woman to have many career choices unless you were determined that you were going to break the mold." Another sixty-something woman shared, "When I was going to school we were told we were going to be teachers, maids or nurses. We weren't aware of other things that we could do." A fifty-two-year-old woman wasn't the only one to indicate her parents played a significant role in directing her choice, "My mother wanted me to be a nurse. It really wasn't my choice. I just went along with it. And, by then, you just did what your parents said you were going to do."

Sometimes being in between social change is confusing and frustrating. On one hand, we, as women, are told not to depend on our man (or society) for economic, emotional or any other support, that we must do this on our own. On the other hand, we have not developed the skills to do this effectively; we have not learned them from our

mothers. They may tell us what NOT to do, but they can't show us how not to do it. When I see young women that are ten years or so younger than me, I am happy for them, but so frustrated for myself. They understand choices and options and the need to do things that are fulfilling to themselves and not others. They appear to have *no* guilt or concept of dimming their own goals and gifts to fit in with what is expected from society.

—Olivia, 29 years old

But even for the young women who have careers, looking for the prince—the man, the ring—isn't one of those quaint old customs of women from the twentieth century. One young woman, 25 years old and emerging from an unfortunate marriage said, "I didn't really love him. It's just all the women my age were getting married, and I felt weird being single. He had plenty of good qualities, and I thought he'd do. He didn't." In Lynn Johnston's syndicated cartoon trip, *For Better and Worse,* the young adult Elizabeth left a holiday party early because she was single among married people, and felt out of place.

And the thirty-something-year-old writer of the popular blog *Break up Babe* reports on a first date, "But seeing as I am now a more evolved person (and because he has not yet asked me on a second date), I have maintained an admirable detachment in this situation, and have not picked out my wedding dress yet."

Good as I Can Be

I wanted to follow the rules established by society even when it wasn't in my best interest. And, even though this 'rule following' thing went so against my nature, I did it anyway. No wonder I was all twisted up inside!

—Olivia, 40 years old

John Taylor Gatto, New York's 1991 *Teacher of the Year*, got amazing results from his students by giving them independent learning projects and turning them loose to work on their own. He found individual workspaces for them, requisitioning broom closets if necessary. The children took to this new idea with relish.

Students who seemed uneducable turned in commendable projects. Gatto said the kids who had the most trouble with the projects were the good kids with good, solid grades. They kept returning to him, unable to get started, because he wouldn't tell them the 'rules.'

We survive adolescence. We move into young adulthood, trying our best to fit in. We want to be good, so we're willing to play by the rules. We run into rules that tell us the world is not as safe for us as it is for men. We don't *really* believe it, but we do, too. If cultural practices encourage exploration and independence in one group of its citizens, and tells another group it's vulnerable and needs protection, what influence will this practice have on voice? I think the group encouraged to be independent and freethinking will likely be more comfortable making choices and stating opinions. The 'protected' group will be less likely to trust themselves. Then there is the busy work of finding and keeping our prince, the one who will validate our self-worth and self-esteem. So much to do as we plunge into life, so much to keep us busy, so much to distract us from noticing in order to fit in and move ahead, we are forgetting something. We are forgetting our voices. We are forgetting our wholeness.

And when we think we have followed the rules, and arrived in that future we've worked so hard to obtain, we will feel something is missing. But we will have forgotten what it is.

CHAPTER SEVEN

If Not Happily Ever After, Then What?

The birth of a first child will affect a woman's internal landscape like an earthquake, followed by a flood, followed by a volcanic eruption. For a man, it will be more along the lines of a heavy thunderstorm.

—Susan Maushart

I guess I imagined a fairy tale life. I think the difference is that every little girl growing up thinks, "I'm not going to be like that."

—Diane, 56 years old

PAMELA JUNE KIMMELL author of *The Mystery of David's Bridge* shared, "When I was 20 I was newly married, the world was my oyster, I just knew that my entire life was going to be filled with happiness, joy, sunshine, flowers, blah blah blah. It wasn't too terribly long before the reality of the world popped that particular bubble." Triggering this response was a question we asked on-line community members. We asked what advice they would give their twenty-something self. Pam explains, "But if I was to give that young woman who I was just one piece of advice, it would be to take off the rose-colored glasses and try to see things as they really are and not how you want them to be.

I really wanted life to be perfect and it wasn't, and I was disappointed.

Like many mothers, mine had taught me as a little girl that the white knight would carry me off to the castle and I'd live happily ever after. I expected that. I wish that I'd been better prepared for ups and downs in life and not expecting all ups!"

Wife Work! Life Work!

And yet, on the other side of the brick wall (as it were), there are a number of equally troubling issues. First among them is the seemingly fathomless capacity of women to 'settle' for whatever it is they think they can get, their collective horror of 'rocking the boat' or, to use one of my mother's favorite expressions, 'pushing their luck.'

—Susan Maushart

My second favorite household chore is ironing. My first being hitting my head on the top bunk bed until I faint.

—Erma Bombeck

In the fairy tale, Cinderella toiled all day for her stepfamily and sat in the ashes at night. When the Prince finally arrived with her glass slipper in his hands, she achieved what her goodness deserved. She was to be Princess, beautiful and cherished, dancing forever under the glittering lights with her true love. Many of the women I interviewed might have warned Cinderella about what was going to happen when she left the dance. Those skills she honed in pre-Prince days were going to come in mighty handy.

When I asked the interviewees about their responsibilities, approximately half reported that they worked outside the home. All the women but two said the children were their primary duty. Whether working full-time or not, most women solely handled domestic chores and children. A fifty-five-year-old woman explained, "My role in the home is to be the mother, wife and companion. I'm just here to make everybody happy." Another shared, "My ex-husband didn't want me to do anything except focus on the children. He wanted me to throw parties for him and be the hostess. I was to have dinner on the table when he got home. Or else."

One woman claimed, "Everything I do is for the children. If I clean the house, it's for them. If it were just me, I wouldn't do it. I'm cleaning for them. And, if they don't show proper appreciation, then you are a martyr. You end up being a victim." She continued by describing the difference in men and women, "Men can do things for themselves, and women do things for other people."

One fifty-year-old described her role, "When I was first married, I was to be a homemaker. Even though I worked outside the home too, I still worked, cleaned, shopped. After the children came along, I had all those duties." A thirty-five-year-old subject shared an interesting observation about work, "It appears to me that the women do the grunt work, and the men get all the credit."

When asked how they felt about performing domestic duties, the majority of the women expressed dislike. A few, however, appeared to enjoy the work or not mind it. Many separated cooking from domestic chores with about half expressing an interest in cooking. A forty-year-old woman said, "With my ex-husband, I always resented doing the domestic chores. He only noticed what I didn't do." Another shared, "I don't enjoy it, but it's something that has to be done. I've been doing some form of housework since I was eight years old, so it has never been a joy." One sixty-two-year-old female said, "It was pure drudgery." Another explained, "I felt all right about doing the work. I always managed to get through it, and it didn't really bother me. I didn't enjoy doing the chores, but really didn't resent them either." A full-time employed subject said, "I didn't enjoy them. I resented them. Sometimes I'd be so tired and put out. It would be 10:00 o'clock before I could get to bed. My husband would already be in the bed snoozing." One sixty-something female took it in stride, "I didn't resent doing the chores. It was just a duty that we were taught to do. It's just something that we do." Another woman required to handle domestic duties as a child explained: "I had to clean house every day and cook."

One woman obviously distraught by the question asked that the recorder be turned off. When it resumed she explained, "I had no childhood. I was expected to do chores from the time I can remember."

It's a small world...But not if you have to clean it.

—Anonymous

Research conducted throughout the English-speaking world continues to show that wives, whether employed or unemployed, perform 70 to 80 percent of the unpaid labor within families.

—Susan Maushart

The Red Queen

Like the Red Queen in Alice in Wonderland who says, "My dear child you have to run everyday so very, very hard just to stay in place."

—Viola, 83 years old

For there is no counterpart to wife work, no reciprocal 'husband-work' driving males to provide caregiving to their female partners at the expense of well-being."

—Susan Maushart

Viola told me, "You've got lots of choices. Today, you can be anything you want to be. But, you've got to experience life. Some days, like the Red Queen, you've got to run and run and never catch up." In *WifeWork*, Maushart tells us, "Females within marriage are strenuously, overwhelmingly, outrageously responsible for the physical and emotional caretaking of males and offspring. Whether they're working for pay part-time or full-time."

I did think that my mother had sacrificed so much.

—Kathy, 35 years old

A woman, by nature of her birth and courtesy of the messages of her culture, may find herself taking on more responsibility than can be managed in a way that promotes health and growth. Many women are drawn at a young age toward marriage and a family, but in today's economic reality, she finds she must also work. Many of us put off our personal desires or interests until much later in life. Who has the time to handle breadwinning pursuits, domestic responsibilities *and* aspirations?

One of my friends has figured out exactly what she wants to do, but can *never* find the time to implement her own, strictly personal goal. After working 8+ hours, hauling the kiddos all around (carpool, sports activities and lessons), cooking supper and cleaning up, there's simply not any more time left in her day. She already gets up before 5:00 a.m. and is too exhausted by 9:00 p.m. to continue.

My sister has struggled more. Her husband is laid back and was always catered to as a child. She said she had to train him. They struggle with finding the right balance. She's getting more assertive and getting help—like a babysitter, etc. She would like for him to help more than he does. I think some men don't think that way—it doesn't enter their minds that they should help.

—Kathy, 35 years old

So many of us, by biology and natural inclination, begin our relationships assuming much of the traditional tasks of a nurturing caregiver. As we get older, and our lives grow more complex, we assume additional duties. We feel as if we are in a no-win bind. If we let go of our old duties, we feel guilty. If we do not let go of our old duties, we grow wrathful and exhausted. The first person to train is ourselves. Our primary task is to take a realistic look at the messages we are giving ourselves. If we can change the messages and believe in that change, more realistic roles will evolve, in which we learn to care for ourselves as if we are as important in our lives as everyone else.

Smart Enough

I moved back to my hometown with my young son after my divorce. I started pounding the pavement, looking for a job, any job. A farm operation was looking for an office clerk. The mechanic was there when I applied, but the farm owner wasn't. "You come back," the mechanic said. "Mr. Campbell, he has in mind to hire a retired man to do this job. But I have been trying to tell him, if he hired a man smart enough to do this bookwork, he's gonna have to pay him something." And I tell you, I went back. I was that desperate.

—Charlene, 51 years old

When I was growing up our society was changing. In the small Southern towns of my childhood, women mostly modeled the roles played by their mothers and grandmothers. Many of them were still stay-at-home wives and mothers. The ones that did work were smart enough to do any bookwork, but they were paid as if they were wives who wandered out of the kitchen into the workplace. Meanwhile, in the cities, women, often with harsh and angry voices, often very rudely, were demanding change, equal opportunities and equal pay for equal work. Feminist. While nobody doubted equality was a good thing, it seemed as if they were demanding women throw the babies out with the bathwater—and that men, even our husbands and helpful co-workers, were vile oppressors, enemies to be punished for their gender. At the time, I dismissed those angry voices. Although I recognized a problem, I couldn't identify with the solutions I heard.

In our homes, parents told daughters we could do great things, and we believed it. But the backdrop we grew up told a different tale. In reality, men made the decisions in many homes, and got the promotions and pay at work.

The women I talked to shared similar experiences. "As far as decision making my husband was in charge," one fifty-plus-year-old woman said. "My mother made the decisions in our family," another reported. "But she was angry that my dad was abdicating his manly responsibilities. He winced a lot, as if they both knew this was not a healthy state of affairs. I felt kind of sick to my stomach when I watched them. And now I find it hard to make a decision my husband might disagree with." And as one cop said on the popular TV show, *Law and Order,* men chase criminals and women babysit the victims. The idea of men as decision-makers is deeply ingrained in our culture.

I knew that I didn't fit the old mold. In my black and white thinking the one being modeled to me was wrong. My misguided beliefs steered me in a long, drawn-out search of something that actually never existed—my ability to have it all, which included the babies, the bathwater, and a husband who was a friend. And that I could do it all without being rude, and by adhering to the Southern Rules I had grown up with. I lived through many troubled years before I realized there must be another way, a better way, a way uniquely mine.

Looking in All the Wrong Places

"I'm a secret back-to-the-lander." She laughs. "Not really, but you know originally this place was going to be a dome or a yurt. I was going to build it out of recycled goodies. Run goats and fowls, and a guinea pig or two, and have a vegetable garden about six acres square.

Then one night, while I was still in the planning stages, I sat down on the beach and thought, Hulme, what do *you* want? Because all these were other people's ideas...nothing wrong with them, but they didn't really fit me.

—Keri Hulme

We spend years building our lives on rotten foundations. It takes years to build new foundations for a new life.

—Marion Woodman

In my closed little world, the only female role model I saw doing something different was my Aunt Kay, who wanted to be an opera star. She had jumped off the traditional wagon and hitched the bus to New York City to find her fame and fortune. Seeing her take a chance and try to be what she wanted to be made me believe I could do anything, too. But, because I knew her well, I also witnessed her struggle. I learned from observation that it wasn't easy to follow your dreams and that dreams had a high cost—separation from family, minimal income and rejections. Even though I wanted to fly high, I wondered if I could accept the price.

Seeing my aunt go out on an adventure, along with my supportive parents and my awareness that I indeed had something special to offer, I looked to my future with very high hopes. During childhood, I had dreamed of being a singer, performer, writer, professional tennis player, photographer, artist. By the time I graduated, I planned on becoming a practicing clinical psychologist, marrying my high school sweetheart, and having three children. And I knew I could have it all and live happily ever after.

Quite possibly my intense struggle with adolescence led me to want to be a therapist. Perhaps I entered the field to find myself.

I spent four years of college and one internship year on a direct path to my goal despite many obvious limitations—for one, I lacked a mathematical and scientific mind. So I was engaged in something that continually pointed out my weaknesses. While working as an intern for a clinical psychologist, I reached the tough conclusion that I was not cut out for the occupation. As I observed and talked to fifth-year residents—students at the brink of fulfilling all the requirements—I realized that I didn't want the prize. For whatever reason, I had taken a misstep and clinical psychologist was not *my* answer. Unfortunately, my hardcore mentors (clinical psychologists and university professors) did not think highly of what would have been a much more fitting direction for me, a master's degree in education with a license to counsel. Without the approval of my authority figures, I didn't see that choice as an option.

Without a goal, I was one lost puppy. Because I felt I needed to do something professionally and had enjoyed my business minor, I decided to complete an MBA.

I enrolled in the program. While no one pushed me to go in that direction, I knew it made my family and husband happy. And once again, with a goal in hand (completing the degree), I had purpose. Getting my MBA was not easy, but I was in familiar territory—a game I could decipher, and my ability as a strategist gave me the edge I needed to do well. While in the program, I searched for a place—consulting, management, higher education, and computers—but all the options seemed wrong. Not knowing where I was going didn't stop me—I had control of the ball and headed for the goal line. After eighteen months, I made it.

More missteps followed. My first real job was in higher education. I found the Registrar's position thanks to my husband's first real spot in college baseball. The college wanted us to be happy and helped me secure the on-campus job that most suited my skills and abilities. But after about six months, I was ready to jump ship. It was during that time I started buying and reading self-help books. The books and my willingness to learn more marked the beginning of my arduous trek toward something different—something better.

A decade later, I had not found any employment that felt right. Not one shoe fit me. Not one. I was tired, scared and angry. I had floundered for years trying to find the place I belonged. By the time I figured it out, I was beyond having a desire to return to school. And therefore, I didn't.

My lost years, those filled with regret and lacking meaning, were the times that pushed me forward—made me search long and hard for something else. Those lost years were lengthy, grueling and very dry. Not only did I *not* understand why I was filled with sadness and longing, I couldn't figure out how to make money either. Reading all the self-help books I could find, I was convinced that my real problem was my failure to find meaningful work. For over a decade, I thought I could fix myself by finding and securing the perfect job most suited to my strengths, talents and skills.

Throughout this time, I usually worked in an established job with specific hours and a set pay rate. With each new position, and there were many, my tolerance time shortened. As soon as I knew the ropes, I felt trapped and had a driving need to escape. I often prayed my husband would get a new job—because when he did, I had a good excuse to quit.

Thank God, Greg's job changes were fairly regular and rescued me many times. There were, however, times when I had to quit on my own.

My readings convinced me that all my feelings of discontentment were because I wasn't doing my life's work—therefore, my life lacked meaning. Confusing the 'meaning' issue, I had mistakenly tied occupation to it, thereby setting myself up to bang into one brick wall after another. Coupled with my inability to make anything happen, I led a painful existence. I didn't know what to do or how to do it. I was all over the map— creating great ideas that continued to die unattended. Occasionally, an idea would take shape and I'd dabble a little, but peace, happiness, and money eluded me. I thrashed around for at least ten years with the perfect job calling me like Shangri La. Never getting closer to finding contentment. The going was tough.

Then my daughter Addy was born. I had to quit worrying about my own illusive path and turn my attention toward caring for someone else. I instinctively knew I needed to figure out how to stay home with my daughter, but our family needed me to produce an income.

In three years I became the happy stay-at-home mother with a part-time job, the old job description of my mother and grandmother's generations that I had rejected so many years ago, and nobody was more surprised than I was at how happy that made me.

Happy to be at home with Addy, happy to take care of her, happy to help with family finances—nothing in the new/old game plan convinced me I didn't have to provide part of the financial support, unlike the generational domestic division I had grown up with.

For the most part I was content. But still I was aware of a hunger that pushed me. I continued seeking for an answer to a question I could not even articulate.

Along the way I experienced a little wake-up call. The first call I can identify came, oddly enough, from a dolphin.

Addy and I had gone to the Science Spectrum to see a dolphin movie. Peering up at the surround screen, it felt as if we were swimming with them. Free. Wild. Unbound. The brilliant colors, dolphin clicks and sighs, cool ocean waters swallowed us. I imagined living in the small little village by the sea, riding my bicycle to the dock every day, then spending my hours swimming and studying magnificent water creatures. The dolphin lady smiled. The dolphin lady exuded joy. The dolphin lady had something I did not.

I was enthralled. Longing for more freedom and joy, I saw the movie as an invitation to make a better life for myself. The movie and its message stayed with me for months. Why couldn't *I* be the dolphin lady featured on the surround screen? No, I didn't imagine dolphins becoming my life's work, but I was determined to seek and find a life that would be as joyful and meaningful as life among the dolphins seemed to be.

Dream Excerpted from My Journal

As I was finishing up the duties assigned to me in my old life, I had a very revealing dream. A former boss opened his office door and asked me to look at the small box in the corner. His office was completely empty except for this box that resembled a standard mailbox. He said, "Allyn, I want you to fit yourself in that box while I'm gone." I agreed and said that I would do it for him. He closed the door and left. I tried for a long time to fit myself in that small box but couldn't do it. No matter how hard I tried the box just wasn't big enough.

Marsha Sinetar, a well-known career consultant and author once said, "Maybe this narrowing of life—the eroding of interests and hope—could be likened to being cooped up in a room that's too small…The only thing that's stopping you is *you*." How true both her thoughts and my dream turned out to be. My final breaking point was at the pinnacle of my professional life at the time. Three months after being named an Associate Dean at a community college, I declared, "No more!" The pay was fabulous, and the position was definitely good for my ego, but the job was choking the life right out of me. Adding to the pressure, I now had a two-year-old daughter whom I suddenly had no energy to care for. It was all too much and with deep regret, I realized I had just eaten the wrong carrot.

The journey to finding what I was *really* looking for wasn't over yet, but I was sure the heavens rejoiced—I finally got some of the message. Immediately I took back a part-time job I had at the college while I regrouped and rested. Within fourteen months, I had started a home-based business and was making almost as much as I had made when I was Dean minus headaches, stress and fatigue. The business, a résumé writing and career consulting startup, was a perfect match. I knew everything about preparing marketing materials, interviewing and convincing an employer to hire me. My knowledge came from my own experiences, numerous interviews and books. I emerged from all those seemingly dead-end paths as a career consultant. I had a tried and proven means to make money that was very practical and inexpensive to launch. Besides that, I enjoyed the work and relished the opportunity to stay at home with my daughter.

After two years, though, the thought of writing another résumé from scratch was nauseating. To change things up a little, I added grant writing—finding a fairly easy way to add more money to my bottom line. That decision prolonged my home-based business for another six months, but by the time Addy was scheduled to go to school full-time, I knew I had to change things. Not interested in returning to a traditional job or a boss, I sought consulting jobs—short-term contracts and commitments.

As luck would have it, a nonprofit company needed an Interim Executive Director to fill in for nine months. I had the skills and personally knew several board members. A deal was quickly sealed. The contract was part-time, but still provided the share that I needed to contribute to the family income.

With income covered, I dropped all my other contracts with résumé and grant writers. I focused on myself. Finally, I was ready to follow my heart. But first, I had to figure out what my *heart* wanted.

The Sparrow's Lesson

We must be willing to get rid of the life we planned, so as to have the life that is waiting for us.

—Joseph Campbell

It was at that point in my life that the *real* work began. I was much like the bird I observed one day and recorded in my journal.

Excerpted from My Journal

I'm watching a sparrow trying to fly past a utility pole. The bird hits the pole, flies up a little higher, and hits the pole again—it keeps going upward, but is taking such small steps. Sometimes, it flies below where its last highest point was.

Aha! It finally reached the top and flew quickly away. From my vantage point, I saw it all. I saw something the little bird couldn't. I realized that it would have been so much easier for the little bird to fly right or left! Hmmmm, I wonder how many times I've done that? I get so focused on one and only one way out of a stressful situation, and then I waste so much time, beating myself up along the way—moving forward at a snail's pace, fretting, worrying, moving backward. And, all I had to do was fly to the right or to the left. All I had to do was fly directly to the destination.

I have to admit that I was afraid. Very afraid. It seemed to me that I had been at the starting gate so many times before, but never seemed to be able to make it pass the first hurdle.

Throughout my life I've been a constant writer. I didn't seek out a degree or pursue it professionally. To start with I wasn't properly educated in my early years. I had the misfortune of having 'English-teacher-turnover' in my small, rural high school, thereby causing many deficits in my knowledge base.

By the time I got to college, I had to be 'fixed.' The experience led me to believe that I was a terrible writer and not *smart* enough to be literary. To this day, I'll tell you I'm not literary. I'm not. It's just that I need to write. It's just that I am pressed to study, research and share. It's just to find out who I am, I must write. To be who I am, I must write.

Coloring Outside the Lines

Sue Monk Kidd explains the all-familiar traits of the Good Little Girl—a role I most assuredly recognize and identify with. Good Little Girls have a "fear of coloring outside the traditional lines." Looking back at my life, I often handed my power over to an authority outside of myself. I thought excelling and pleasing others constituted love. Or rather, that if I did things the 'right' way, I would be loved. I would fit into this world. By allowing others to define me, I would belong. How quickly I would suddenly feel lost...as if I had lost myself. I lived a life that masked my true feelings and thoughts, and this trained me to be completely focused on the thoughts of others—not only did I try to interpret them, but I tried to meet every need. Kidd spoke of following the path of least resistance, of trying to live a safe and comfortable life. Confrontation was avoided at all costs. Making peace was the primary focus. To make peace, I had to sacrifice myself as well as my own needs.

Why would I do this? So many of us go through life this way. Why? When we don our masks at an early age, when we see our worth in pleasing others, we are too busy looking out to external influences to notice what is going on inside. We don't know what we want, and if we do, and it doesn't come with a big stamp of approval, our heart's desire feels too selfish, foolish and dangerous to pursue.

Luckily, I also had space to step back, take stock. I saw I had been living the life of the princess. I would please the authority—and not a cruel authority, either. Then I would be allowed to live happily ever after. Not.

Instead, I was miserable, without understanding why. Guilty that I felt so bad when life was essentially good. What I had failed to understand is authority resides in each of us. When we relinquish it, we relinquish our own hopes and dreams, our life's purpose.

When we claim that authority, nourish it, follow it, we realize our true calling. No matter what we choose to do, we have claimed the right to be Queen.

CHAPTER EIGHT

When the Princess Takes Her Poison

When Enough Isn't Enough

What is this terrible starving in an addiction? It's as though our whole civilization is feeding the hunger, not to satisfy, but to make us hungrier. There is a sense of I want more, more, more of—something... Then the addiction becomes a tyrant. Its voice is that of a starving, lost child: "I want, I want, I want, and I am going to have."

—Caroline Knapp

I remember being in the 4th grade and having to weigh. We had to weigh in class—it was kilometers. I weighed the same as my tall, skinny friend and I remember thinking, "What's wrong with me?"

—Kathy, 35 years old

HE SNOW WHITE of the Disney movie is the perfect Good Little Girl with no shadow self. She is the cheerful Momma and housekeeper to seven dwarfs, with nary a complaint about coal dust or other people's clutter for her to clean. Grumpiness merely makes her laugh. She even dances while she cleans, with the only thought about herself being that time when the prince will come. Then she eats the poisoned apple brought to her by her wicked stepmother and falls down as if dead.

As girls, many of us strive to be the princess. We aim to please. We will perform. We must be perfect. And for some of us, food becomes as deadly as the stepmother's apple. It becomes our first addiction, our first symptom.

I was a healthy child. I never thought much about weight. My mother made sure we ate good, wholesome foods. Our after-school snack was cauliflower and curry dip, which I liked. We didn't have desserts at meals. Treats were reserved for special occasions. Cokes were only allowed on Saturday afternoons. Sometimes seconds were allowed during meals, and sometimes not.

My body began changing in fifth grade. First, there was the hair *down there,* and soon after my breasts began developing. I began having periods shortly after my eleventh birthday. The changes were frightening, but my mother continually reassured me nothing was wrong. She supplied books to fill in the missing pieces.

In the sixth grade, we had been studying measurements, so the teacher brought in a scale. She was going to weigh us all. I hadn't weighed except at the doctor's office, so I was interested in seeing what my weight would be. One by one we stood on the scale, and the teacher would call out the weight. We were having lots of fun making comments and comparing ourselves to our peers. My name was called. I hopped on the scale and looked down.

"Oh, my," the teacher said. "Allyn weighs triple digits."

I don't remember how the other students reacted, but I was mortified. I saw my weight in a bad light. And didn't like it.

Starting with junior high, I tried to live on tuna salad and Diet Rite™ so I could achieve the shape of the ideal woman. I tried every diet I discovered. Cabbage soup. Grapefruit. Cambridge. My freshman year of college, I gained the common Freshman 20. But, with the help of all my diets, I quickly lost it.

In college I assisted a psychology professor studying body image. This was at Ole Miss, the citadel of maidenly beauty. In most instances, beautiful, thin women lined up to grossly exaggerate their body size. Meaning, their perception of how *big* they were was unrealistic.

Surprisingly, many of the men I tested erred too—they consistently thought their *shoulders* were bigger!

I do not know how the overall numbers played out or what hypothesis was being considered. I simply got extra credit for helping the psychologist collect the data while having the opportunity to look at image from the perspective of others. But, the frightening thing to me was how *off-base* these beautiful, healthy women were about their own appearance.

In hindsight, I know my view was twisted too. My interest in the subject matter made me more aware of the symptoms of eating disorders, and I spotted the signs everywhere. In my college dorm bathroom the sounds, smells and splatters told the tale. In my sorority dining room, I watched the afflicted girls push food around on their plates instead of eating it.

It was all right there in my face. The saddest part, though, was I had the affliction and didn't even know it. My problem was *not* on a grand scale, but I denied myself food and followed crazy restrictive diets.

I also shared personality characteristics of people with eating disorders. I wanted approval and needed to please others even if my actions were detrimental to myself. I needed control over every situation that arose. I needed to be a perfect young woman living in a perfect world.

Attending graduate school was particularly hard for me. I had created this scary little place in my head that housed only highly intelligent people—they all wore glasses, had only intellectual conversations, sat around and drank cappuccino. I was scared to death by the time I arrived—afraid that I wasn't going to measure up or be good enough. Of course, in reality, I found some of those students, but I also found students like me—students who had to study and weren't pontificating on the next economic summit or technical invention. But, still, I worried and stressed about my inability to finish or complete the required tasks.

This self-doubt plagued me from adolescence to my early thirties. Always afraid the dark side would emerge and show the real me, I didn't reveal my true self. I wanted to be perfect.

After my child was born, I couldn't lose that final twenty pounds. I kicked myself up and down with my verbal assaults. I would measure myself on the 'good girl' scale each day. Was I good today? Well, what did I eat? If I was *really* sticking to the low-carb fare, then I was doing great. I could usually maintain a low-carb diet for five to seven days and then I couldn't take it anymore. The stepping out occurred gradually and began on a Friday unless I just couldn't talk myself out of starting on a Thursday night. Sometimes I could return to my hardcore low-carb program and sometimes I could not.

Going over the 'highest-weight-reached' mark, I worried I would not be able to make myself return to what I considered an acceptable size. I couldn't seem to control myself enough to get to the desired weight, so why should I think I could ever stop gaining weight once I started slithering down the slippery slope? It was scary, and something that always lurked in the back of my mind.

For me, the weight issue was about control. If I struggled so with just a little extra poundage, what would happen to me later? Would I just keep expanding? Could I continually manage to keep my weight below a certain level, or one day would it just keep on going and going? Would I eventually lose control? Could I really call what had happened to my body a success?

Meanwhile, my long lost five-year-old self threw fits. "I want. I want. I deserve. Don't make me give up everything fun." Maybe it was the five-year-old child in me wishing to escape the tyrannical parent in the form of cultural rules, while the parent within me constantly questioned my neediness to follow those very rules. No win. All the wanting part of me could do was whine and cry, desperate for recognition, desperate for approval, desperate for validity. With no other means to comfort my needy, shadow self, I usually succumbed and gave that self the best substitute I had food that never comforted me because it couldn't. Food was wanting too much. Food was poison, and proof of my imperfection.

So many of the women I interviewed also felt their weight was tied to their emotions. Many of them used food for emotional reasons. With it they could give love (and receive it in exchange for goodness—theirs and the good food), suppress pain (and give themselves a measure of comfort they could not find elsewhere), or to celebrate (with their good friend food). But food makes a treacherous lover.

Some women described a tortuous relationship with food, one filled with denial, obsession and an out-of-control appetite. Many of the conversations about food I had with women during the course of my research reminded me of the psychology experiments I helped administer while in college. I imagined legions of beautiful women reaching out for the apple poisoned by legions of cultural messages that told them they just weren't good enough to be Queen.

Not perfect enough is an issue of self-esteem. Some of the women I talked to reported issues with self-esteem or confidence. One fifty-five-year-old subject said, "I think it was because I had low self-esteem until I was 35. I had no self-worth. I knew God loved me, but I didn't know I was worth anything."

What is it that makes us feel less than enough?

When Food Isn't Food

Many times food isn't about satisfying hunger and refueling the body. A forty-something-year-old subject said, "At mealtime I heard about the starving children in Ethiopia. With those poor children in mind, I was told to clean my plate." I think my starving country was India. I heard about them in many kitchens and dining rooms while growing up. Numerous women reported hearing about the poor starving children, but interestingly, each had a different country to worry about.

Part of what adds to our already overtaxed schedule is our ideas about what we 'must' and 'should' do. *Must* and *should* typically are tied up with pleasing others versus the self. I must clean up this house because someone might drop by unexpectedly. I must clean my plate because children are starving in India. Many of us create our lists of things that should or must be done because of the self-imposed rules we created to organize our little world. I shouldn't miss my walk today or I'll get fat. I should take my daughter to the park, or I will be a bad mom. I must go to the store because we're out of ketchup and the kids can't eat anything without ketchup. "Should, should, should…must, must, must."

While I was working on this book, the *shoulds* and the *musts* got in my way—slowed me down because my rules required that certain things be done before I started my real work. Little things like cleaning the house, cooking dinner, handling administrative tasks. Mostly the *shoulds* that blocked my path involved domestic duties.

But, also I got in my way. My *shoulds* and *musts* could stop my writing—my flow. My *shoulds* and *musts* could make me act right, which inevitability meant help me stray off course.

The Hungry Mother

For many women, food and self-worth is a generational struggle. They had hungry mothers, the caregivers who gave and gave and gave, then had little way to replenish themselves.

Forty-five-year-old Cynthia, a writer, shared a touching essay about her mother she wrote from a child's perspective:

Mommy doesn't see me. She doesn't know I'm here. I see her. We're in the kitchen. Mommy is sitting at the table—the box of ice cream bars next to her. She is lost in her thoughts as she munches away on one and then another. It's a rhythmic motion. Fluid. She keeps eating, eyes staring straight ahead until the ice cream bars are gone. All gone. Every last one of them. Watching her makes me sad. I wanted one!

I consider telling her that I'd like to have one. Or, would she maybe save one for me? But, I know that I should not interfere. I know not to impede the forward motion. Doing so would send all the anger my way—the anger being suppressed by ice cream bars. Anger that I rarely see as it is wrapped up tightly. Controlled. Very controlled. Her actions screamed at me, "More, more. I need more. Is this all there is?"

Another subject shared, "Food was a touchy subject in my house. I was warned that having a big appetite was bad for you. I wasn't allowed to have seconds or desserts. My mother told me one thing, but modeled another. I knew I better hide my treats, if I wanted them for myself because when my mother started eating, she couldn't stop. She'd stuff my candy or cupcakes down her throat. She'd grab for more."

When your life is making sure other people have more, what's left to give yourself? Food, easily available, can chemically act on your brain to soothe your pain, and you can still drive the car and pick up the kids at school without putting anyone's life at risk. Pass the cupcakes. What you are doing is feeding yourself the apple, with the same intention of the Wicked Stepmother. You are trying to poison the Princess who wanted more, who wanted Happy Ever After, who, if she found her voice, would destroy the safety of the Kingdom, which is the only home you know.

When the Princess Doesn't Die

When a woman is exhorted to be compliant, cooperative, and quiet, to not make upset or go against the old guard, she is pressed into living a most unnatural life—a life that is self-blinding...without innovation. The worldwide issue for women is that under such conditions they are not only silenced, they are put to sleep. Their concerns, their viewpoints, their own truths are vaporized.

—Clarissa Pinkola Estés

My dad never thought my interest in sports was meaningful. He thought it was a waste of my time. And, while he never articulated that thought, the emotion was present, and I continually picked up on it. Plus, he was always gone. So, I either overachieved to please and get attention, or I got into trouble (sneaking out, drinking, smoking) to get attention. I also suffered from digestive problems and acne.

—Sydney, 40 years old

My dad constantly praised me. If I needed him, he was there for me. He was proud of my achievements and told me so. But still the cultural messages worked their curse. While they did not vaporize me, they certainly made it appear essential parts of my nature were dead. I was not good enough, smart enough, pretty enough…for whom? Who knows? But, all those years spent *not* being myself was not only emotionally painful, but physically painful as well. Spastic colon and acne are all physical manifestations of stress. I didn't make the connection, though, until after the pain had abated.

In high school, the doctor told me to go home and eat to avoid additional stress from dealing with my digestive complications in school. He told my principal that I had to go home every day to eat my lunch—in a quiet, relaxed environment. My classmates, however, didn't understand the need or reason. I looked like everything was okay. Why did I get a special favor?

To this day my brother-in-law still kids me about my lunchtime breaks. "I'd look out my math class window and there you'd go, strolling off to your car to go home," he reminds me. I haven't forgotten. What the other kids saw as privilege, I saw as necessary.

There were instances in my life when the pain reached unbearable levels. During one attack, mother decided I needed medical attention and drove me to the hospital emergency room.

As I aged and moved from an adolescent to a young adult, my bouts eased. Spastic colon disturbed me some, but mostly with each passing year my stomach and intestines improved.

Acne came next. Initially, the attacks were minor, quickly taken care of by the dermatologist. Each year, the bouts worsened leaving me with red, angry bumps and then scars. I continued to visit dermatologists, but their magic stopped working. I remember one woman in Texas telling me, following her examination of my skin, "Well, this is absolutely the worst I've seen in awhile." I left her office destroyed. Yet another time, a male doctor told me he thought I might have more testosterone than other women. Did I mind taking some tests to find out? I signed up immediately. My insurance company would cover the cost and maybe this would be my answer. If the good doctor knew the cause, then he could help me. I anxiously waited for the results.

"Yes. You have more testosterone than most."

I was thrilled. "Okay, so what do we do about it?"

He didn't have any answers. I was merely his guinea pig—used for scientific research. But I took his diagnosis under advisement. If I were going to be 'whole,' I was also going to be under stress for not fitting in. If I were going to fit in, I had to stuff my Shadow Box even fuller. But those parts of myself I could not accept were going to get my attention, knotting my intestines, ripping at my skin. Holding the poison in, erupting.

Five years of treatment that included powerful drugs, like Acutane, and numerous doses of antibiotics didn't solve the problem. Even though my acne stints would last for ten more years, I quit going to dermatologists. I found that my bumps responded the same whether treated or not. My inflamed face was something I had to endure. The red, angry bumps were hard to wear. So were the leftover scars. I made myself look others in the eye even when I felt ugly, dirty, nasty. I cried a lot during flare-ups.

My other bugaboo, spastic colon is now called Irritable Bowel Syndrome (IBS).

Interestingly, researchers are looking into what causes IBS. Common enough to turn heads, the University at Buffalo and the University of Wisconsin Parkside joined forces to investigate the problem. According to researcher, Jeffrey M. Lackner, "Most people who have IBS have a kind of submissive, nonassertive style; difficulty making their needs known to others; and difficulty being firm with others." Damian McNamara reported Dr. Lackner's findings, "People with IBS ranked higher for being nonassertive and socially inhibited." In yet another interview he claimed, "It appears that people who have trouble making their needs known are more likely to suffer."

As I reached my mid-thirties, the attacks lessened and eventually, for the most part, disappeared. My acne was subdued enough I could invest in medical cures and miracle products to repair the ravages on my skin.

I do not think it is a coincidence that the more I searched for a better life, the more I practiced naming my desires and working toward them, the less I was troubled with IBS and acne. No wonder the doctors couldn't 'cure' me. There was no magic cure for any of my ailments—the relief came from living a more authentic life.

I realized my struggles with food—appetite—were from an ancient tradition, strict and unforgiving cultural messages dictating that women who deserved protection had to send parts of their true natures into hiding. Excess weight turns into protective armor. To protect our soul the body takes on weight, or acne, or a rash or some other external symptom to protect us.

Author and researcher, Marion Woodman says, "The truth is the body is the best friend we have, although most of us think it's our worst enemy. It's like a donkey that gets beaten again and again, but it still tries to hold whatever balance it can."

Woodman said she hated her body. Despised it. At a very low point in her life she had an out-of-body experience. She saw her anorexic-wracked body on the floor—a floor covered in vomit and other bodily excrements. In her head, she visualized herself kicking that body. Calling it names. Cursing it. Suddenly she realized that she wouldn't treat a dog like that. She wouldn't treat her own dog, Duffy, like that. The intense level of self-loathing she had for herself couldn't be seen until she viewed it from a different perspective, from a place where she no longer identified 'that' body with her own being.

Our bodies, much like the donkey or dog referred to by Marion Woodman, are just trying to keep the peace, the balance. Our body protects us, houses our spirit, gives us illnesses, takes on weight only with the instinctive goal of healing us—with the singular intent of helping us return to our glory. If we take the body literally, then how can what we feed it or give it be satisfying what we hunger for? How? If we were only interested in making our stomachs full, then wouldn't our desire to stop eating be prompted by a full tummy?

An insatiable appetite has nothing to do with our body.

The Unlived Life

Truth is like the sun. You can shut it out, but it ain't going away.

—Elvis Presley

When I began tracing my discontent back through my life, I discovered everything was upside down. Conforming to the cultural messages I felt as disoriented as the jilted lover in Dolly Parton's song, *The Grass is Blue.* The messages the culture sent me about my reality were not my reality…no more than "rivers flow backward" or "mountains are level." The appearance I met everywhere I turned was not the truth. I was told to be myself, but only the self that would meet rigid standards of the rules. "I'm perfectly fine," I would try to tell my Shadow Self, the one I sent into hiding, "I don't miss you."

Marion Woodman has another name for the Shadow Self—Unlived Life. When we crave, when we eat when we're not hungry, when we drink to pretend we're happy, when we shop because that new pair of shoes is not needed but is essential to our identity, we are trying to satisfy the Shadow Self, the Unlived Life.

Addictions come in many *wants:* drugs, nicotine, gambling, sex, shopping, eating, lying, time spent on the computer or diet colas. We are looking for something external to fill the emptiness and mask the pain of the Self we have denied.

But, I was a spy in the world of happy eating, always hungry, or stuffed, but never full. Luckily, I was still drinking at the time.

—Anne Lamott

Sometimes when we have to choose, there aren't any choices. It's just either this not right thing, or that one. It's the Law of Shitty Choices.

—Olivia, 55 years old

Feeding our addictions provides a way to stuff down, if only momentarily, frustration, anger and remorse. When we perceive choice as submission or rebellion, we feel like we're faced with no choices or bad choices, which might even be worse. Feeding the addiction becomes a way to have some choice, to feel like we have enough control to bring something good into our lives. Then we immediately feel out of control.

Marion Woodman has another idea about our need for food or the unquenchable appetite. "Well, the soul is starving; it's true, because it's not being recognized, and it's being continually starved. They (women) then try to feed it (soul) with food, which usually symbolizes the loving mother who can accept them as they are."

The need to stuff down our emotions is an affliction shared by anyone whose approval depends on following other people's rules, on sending parts of yourself into hiding to conform to cultural imperatives.

When you feel you are loved only when others approve of your behavior, your appearance, and even your thoughts, when you give and give and give and never ask, when you don't make the rules and you don't like them, then you seek something that can give you a tiny bit of instantaneous satisfaction, something to disguise your gaping loss—the loss of who you might have been.

Donna Henes, author of *The Queen of My Self* writes, "If we ignore our unresolved problems, chronic irritants, and burning resentments, we can be sure that they will surface as toxic stress that can cause cancer, heart attacks, substance abuse, depression and other debilitating and life-threatening problems. How successful we handle our changes now will determine the quality of our health and well being for all of our future years. Our life literally depends on it."

Television talk shows highlight troubled women and men, daily featuring individuals on the brink of bankruptcy, battling with obesity or hanging out in dangerous places seeking sex or drugs. The success stories are typically portrayed as intense battles with the self to overcome and to conquer the demons that ultimately destroy any shred of the remaining goodness of life.

The answer lies within taming the fears and digging deep enough to uncover the cause of the pain—if only enough to at least find questions such as how did things get to be such a mess. With the right questions, answers appear. With awareness comes release and healing.

Sometimes greeting the demons by name is all that's required to see them for what they are—parts of the Unlived Life. Other times, it takes more. It takes things like forgiveness, surrender and release. The pain is real. The drug of choice is real. The healing is also real.

There is nothing inherently wrong with a hot fudge brownie with whipped cream, or a glass of wine or two or three, but it behooves us all to look at how we consume, and why. Why do you drink? Why do you drink in excess? What does the alcohol do? How does it make you feel?

These are the questions I had to ask myself. "What does it do for me?" Again referring to Marion Woodman's large body of work, I discovered many interesting passages about addiction. In one book, *Conscious Femininity* (excerpted from *Family Secrets: Life Stories of Adult Children of Alcoholics*) the interviewer describes well-respected researcher and psychiatrist, Carl Jung's views on addiction. Jung worked closely with an alcoholic, Rowland H., whose sobriety led to the establishment of Alcoholics Anonymous (AA). Jung wrote: "It was no accident alcohol is also called 'spirits' and said that the alcoholic's thirst for alcohol is equivalent to the soul's thirst for 'the union with God.' Alcohol in Latin is spiritus, and you use the same word for the highest religious experience as well as for the most depraving poison. The helpful formula then is: spiritus contra spiritus. It's an alchemical formula. It takes spirit to counter spirit."

A soul seeking comfort in a bottle or pill is looking for something so much deeper than relief. If you believe Marion Woodman, it's a longing for spirit and deeper connection with God. It is an erroneous attempt to feed the Unlived Life, the Shadow Self, when what is needed is light and air.

I can't for the life of me determine the trigger. I want. I want. I need. I deserve. Therefore, I eat. I drink. But, I still want more. Somebody once told me eating past fullness was a way to quiet the connection with the Divine. The *more* I eat or drink the *less* I hear. I can keep the truth from surfacing if I bury it. Bury it with appetite, longing and then, finally, guilt for even having the appetite. What's the desire trying to squelch or fill?

—Olivia, 40 years old

There is a crack, a crack in everything. That's how the light gets in.

—Leonard Cohen

And, I finally got it. The veil dropped. I got that I am as mad as the hatter.

—Anne Lamott

As children, we discover being fully who we were born to be is risky. We hide those unacceptable parts away; pretend they don't exist. Still those hidden parts call to us. Won't let us rest.

We buried the Shadow Self because it frightened us. How can we let it out now? Better to grab the chocolate bar, the glass of wine, the new boyfriend, the great new blouse.

Addictions let us do that. The present is not the moment of choice; it's a place to avoid the now. That's why we can postpone eating healthily or quitting smoking until Monday. Pain isn't felt if you are not living it. Pain doesn't hurt as badly when it's pushed down; shoved to the future, lost in the past. If we did live life in the moment, we would come face to face with the Unlived Life.

If we're lucky, our old life will break. It simply won't work anymore. We will decide not to mask the pain anymore. We will invite the Shadow Self to emerge. Oh, we will shiver, we will cry. We might rage. So much anger, so much fear. We will do it, because after all that striving to be the Good Girl, we find we're as mad as the hatter in somebody else's upside-down world.

Hooray for things that cannot hold, that must break, because if we hold steady, if we refuse to fall asleep again, if we let the craziness pass, we will discover there was nothing scary there at all. Everywhere some way of being is not working, there is the crack that lets the light in.

It is there the Lived Life, abundant and joyous, will shine forth. We will no longer be princesses felled by an attractive poison. We will be Queens, capable of abundant giving because we abundantly accepted all that we are.

98

CHAPTER NINE

Changing the Contract

I too sat in the midst of many selves. The Pleaser, the Performer, the Perfectionist—my trinity of P's. I was learning how closely these old roles were connected to another powerful role that I played out: the Good Little Girl. She was the part of me that had little self-validation or autonomy, who tended to define life by others and their expectations, by collective values and projections. As a woman I sometimes felt that I had been scripted to be all things to all people. But when I tried, I usually ended up forfeiting my deepest identity, my own unique truth as God's creature.

—Sue Monk Kidd

OUR CURRENT PATRIARCHAL social structure—the Monarchy— has been in place for thousands and thousands of years—it's pre-historic. According to my research, there is no real evidence that a true matriarchal society ever existed. And there are real reasons for the existence of a patriarchal structure, based on survival of the species, DNA, hormones, and socialization. Conditional love reinforces it all, and continues to refine the monarchy with localized customs (most of which have counterparts in other areas of the world) such as my Southern Rules or my sub-cultural influences.

Let's face it. Governing rules suit the most powerful, though there is always wiggle room in the governing rules for those who are not. Just because there are reasons for the social structure developing the way it did doesn't mean those rules were ever right for everyone or all the time—women or men.

And our world has been on a fast course for change for quite a while. Technology has changed the landscape of society. Having many children now threatens the economic well-being of the family, rather than enhances it. The division of labor no longer has a basis in a hunting/gathering or a heavy labor/tend the babies' way of life. While research indicates men and women's brains may process information in different ways, in the end, they do get to the same information. What's most problematic in gender roles in today's society are the messages we have carried from the past, which tell us we must relate to one another in old ways in a new landscape.

A small girl wants to be just like her mother. She slips her feet into her mother's high heels, and smears her face with lipstick. If she can reach her mother's razor, she is likely to take the skin off her own leg.

As we grow older, we slip into our mother's life. The majority of the women I talked to admired their mothers and wanted to be at least partially like them. Many women had taken stock of what didn't work in their mothers' lives and attempted to change things for themselves.

Many of us discovered the rules have changed, and what worked for our mother has become ill-fitting for us, like shoes that are too small. As one woman told me, "We took bits and pieces of our mother (my sister and I), but I didn't want to be like her. My mother was always very hard on people, and I try not to do that." She continued, "But, quite frankly, she was probably hardest on herself. A fever of 102 degrees wouldn't stop her from hosting a Christmas dinner for sixty people." A woman born in 1964 shared, "It was important for me to be different. She was one of those women that when her husband rattled a tea glass, she'd jump up and fill it. I never wanted to be classified as someone's mother or someone's wife. All I saw her do was take care of other people. No, I didn't want to be like that."

A fifty-five-year-old warned me, "But if you are saying that I'm not going to live how my mother lived, then what you have is a void. You're not going toward something." Another woman laughed while saying, "I knew when I was very little that I didn't want to be like my mother. But, the danger in that is that you lose your role model." Then she said, "My sister and I only recently started talking about how mother was a wonderful person. It was just that she was mad all the time while we were growing up."

A woman in her late fifty's summed it up, "I tried not to be like my mother and now I've stopped fighting it."

For most of us, our mother's world would become our reality, even the parts that crimped our own lives, even the parts that hurt.

The Warriors, Pioneers and Trailblazers

Well, I've wrestled with reality for 35 years, doctor, and I'm happy to state I finally won out over it.

—Elwood P. Dowd

What is needed today is a change in contract, and that never comes without confusion. Most of us take the path of least resistance. We fit our square peg into a round hole. We wrestle with reality. But change does occur. Human beings are no longer possessed by others; women can own property and vote. In the United States, children are no longer exploited in adult jobs. People are not excluded from livelihood due to race.

The harbingers of change often make names for themselves. They are seen as more aggressive. Frankly, they are viewed often rude and as not playing nicely.

We know them. They stick out bigger than the rest of us. We know their message and may or may not believe in their cause. Typically abrasive, they often offend many people, and at first what they do seems to make situations worse. But then, change occurs, and we cannot imagine returning to the old ways.

An HBO Original movie, *Iron Jawed Angels*, featured the life of Alice Paul, one of the leading individuals responsible for the ratification of the 19th Amendment (women suffrage) to the United States Constitution. Falsely imprisoned, Alice and her supporters suffered at the hands of authority. President Woodrow Wilson's advisors sent a psychiatrist to the prison psychiatric ward to evaluate the mental and emotional capabilities of Ms. Paul with the hopes of committing her to long-term care. When repeatedly questioned about her sanity, the psychiatrist said, "Courage is often mistaken for insanity."

So what's really insanity—that women should want to vote, or that they should not be allowed to vote? Pick your century.

I was trying…to lead a conventional life, for that was how I was brought up, and it was what my husband wanted of me. But one can't build little white picket fences to keep the nightmares out.

—Anne Sexton

I felt like there was somewhere else I was supposed to be. Something else I was supposed to be doing. I was intellectually and emotionally stifled.

—Diane, 56 years old

When conditions that created the rules change, the ruled can feel crazy. And when they try to change the rules, they may feel even crazier. Everywhere they turn, they hear, "Stop this nonsense," because we, like all other species, view change as a threat. How many times does an individual striving to make sense of the world around her, deciding she's not crazy, the rules are crazy, hear, "If ain't broke, don't fix it?" Yet, she knows something is breaking, and she fears it is herself.

You go through a painful process of severance, similar to the Hero's Journey, because you are no longer part of the tribal mind. 'For whosoever will save his life shall lose it,' Jesus said. You have broken away

from the general mind-set, and the group is likely to perceive your individuation—like anything new or different from the status quo—as a fundamental threat to its own unity. Ironically, as in the case of these great teachers, severance from one's personal tribe can lead to something beneficial to the survival of the universal human tribe. The great mystics—Abraham, Moses, the Buddha, Jesus, Muhammad—all shared a common fate of abandonment and separation from their tribe early in their mission...

—Caroline Myss

It Takes Two to Tango

Now you ask a group of young women on a college campus, "How many of you are feminists?" Very few will raise their hands because young women don't want to be associated with it anymore because they know it means male-bashing and being a victim, and it means being bitter and angry.

—Christina Hoff Sommers

As I wrote this book, a friend kept asking, "All this about patriarchy was said in the suffrage movement at the beginning of the last century, and again in the 60s and 70s...very loudly. Why didn't it take then? Why didn't you hear it? Why are we having to repeat this message?"

The story of the Monarchy has been told since civilization began. "Once upon a time there lived a king..." It seems when it's time to change a narrative, many elements have to be discarded, and all the landmarks disappear from the future. In her poem *Mother's Day*, Nicaraguan poet Daisy Zamora acknowledged her children might want a different mother, a pretty, happy mother who didn't disturb anyone with her problems. But, she told them, "I wanted to be myself—and for a woman that's hard." She continued by telling them what all mothers know, "I cannot tell you that I know the road. Often I lose my way." In spite of difficulties and without a compass to direct her travels, she advanced, like we advance, with the hope our children will pull into a distant port after we've "been lost at sea."

In a sense, the loudest feminists mothered us with their strident, often pompous, and authoritarian voices. Although my reaction meant shunning the message, without them this book would not have been written. I would not have attained enough space from the Monarchy and from my Southern Rules to know exactly where to start looking at the pain and how to heal it.

We were high on the women's movement; the voices from New York were like foghorns saving us in the night, but they also frightened us because they were so strident.

—Anne Lamott

We have arrived in that distant port, one not imagined by our trailblazers of the Second Wave of Feminism. They used many planks to build their boats to bring us here. The messages I heard seemed to require I amputate parts of myself to save myself. "Avoid the traditional arrangement of marriage. Working outside the home is the Utopia that will save all women. Staying at home with the kids is a poor, stupid and unfulfilling way to spend one's time. As victims and secondary citizens, women need to be rescued." I wanted choices, not another know-it-all's voice telling me what I should or should not do. I didn't want rescuing. I wanted the tools to make an intelligent and fulfilling life with not another party line, but with my own story in place.

Those Warrior Feminists brought with them a warring mentality—*us* against *them. Women* against *Men. Feminists* against *Traditionalists.* Let's face it. There had to be more in play than just 'men were physically bigger, so they got to make the rules' as a basis for the social structure that nourishes us and gives us so much grief. We can't discard biology, any more than we should make biology the measure by which all roles are assigned. We all have similar desires: to be loved, appreciated, accepted and happy, and to seek our purpose in life, and fulfill it. It's just that under the old messages of the Monarchy, under the Southern Rules, men seem to have permission to seek these things—such as believing it's all right to get their needs met without having to lose themselves.

I always thought being female was the short end of the stick. If you were playing cards, that wouldn't have been the hand you wanted. Men just seemed to have more enjoyment and less worry. That's what was modeled to me. The guys got the better deal.

—Deedra, 40 years old

When Different is Dangerous

We have to dare to be ourselves, however frightening or strange that self may prove to be.

—May Sarton

In Madeleine L'Engle's *A Wrinkle In Time,* Meg Murray must travel to the distant planet Camzotz to save her brother, Charles Wallace, from the evil entity, IT. On earth, Charles Wallace is different from the other kids, and they make fun of him, which frustrates and embarrasses Meg. But he is her brother, and she must save him. IT is gobbling up universes, one planet at a time, making everything exactly alike, making everyone conform to IT's own rhythms, under the premise that when everyone is alike, everyone will be equal.

In the movie based on the book, the villagers all wore the same clothes in the same colors, all the while bouncing a ball or tapping their fingers to the same, rhythmic beat. Those violating the law of sameness underwent reprogramming. The citizens who bought into the concept of equality as defined by IT sought sameness. Those that were different were reported to the proper authorities. Those that were different were 'not' equal. They were viewed as sick or criminal, and needed to be fixed.

In one eerie scene, all the children are outside during the *playing hour.* All are playing by themselves, and all are doing something to produce the culturally accepted rhythmic beat. The one child who deviates is escorted to Central Intelligence for fixing. Throughout the ordeal, the children are warned if they act out they will be reported to the proper authorities. Everyone accepts the message 'different is unacceptable.'

In order to save Charles Wallace from the all-powerful IT, Meg needed to remember what she had that IT didn't have. "Like and equal are *not* the same," she said.

Viewing like and equal as the same introduces a paradox. On the surface, the argument that the two meanings are similar appears valid, but upon further investigation, it is obvious they are not. Equality, then, does not require likeness. In our world being different does not result in governmental reprogramming. But the tendency to conform is strong. Just like in the movie, the odd character is ostracized. The people who act like everyone else and talk like everyone else are embraced, but have lost their individuality.

What are little boys made of? *Frogs and Snails and Puppy Dog Tails.* What are little girls made of? *Sugar and Spice and Everything Nice.*

Must boys be boys and girls be girls? Certainly we don't want to force boys to be girls and girls to be boys, but what about the ones of us who long to bounce the ball differently? Our feminist mothers, the ones who put out to sea, opened so many doors for us. But freedom is *not* about sexual partners, freedom from childcare, power at work, economics, freedom from domestic chores. It's not about disowning our birth mothers, and grandmothers. It's not about suppressing our biology.

It's about being yourself, listening and marching to your internal voice, loving and nurturing yourself. About knowing your own choices are legitimate, and thus being free to accept the choices your significant other and children make about what makes life purposeful for them.

In our home, I am very much the 'keeper' of the house. I do all the cooking and am responsible for the cleaning. I hated deep cleaning, and even when we didn't have any spare money, I usually hired someone to come weekly to do those chores. In our marriage, it's always been my job. The more I contribute financially, the more help I can hire. If it were my husband's job, he'd 'pay' someone to do the chores he didn't want to do. He handles the yard, so our domestic chores are split along gender lines. He vacuums and washes clothes occasionally.

These are our choices. If they no longer work for either of us, we know we can back up and look for other ways of handling them. It's when the messages are engrained about what we are supposed to do, rather than doing what works for us, that tradition becomes a trap.

Our old cultural messages told us we must be like everyone else, divided down rigid lines of male and female. Our feminist teachers said we must be alike, man and woman, to be equal. Now we are setting out to sea, again with no charts, no way of knowing what shore our children will arrive on.

The new ship is built on inclusion. We have set out to teach one another to create our own realities. We are learning to accept differences. There's a paradox, though, because we are 'we' and therefore alike, but within 'we,' each individual is very different, each having his or her own balance of yin and yang, male qualities and female qualities. Some have more yang while others have more yin. By marrying those warring parts, we become whole and part of the universal 'we.' No longer at war, we individually find peace.

The greatest gift we can offer our girls and boys is to instill in them an understanding of this paradox. Individuality is important, but more significant is the acceptance and understanding that differences are to be cherished and rewarded. Individuality is a gift. Talents from God are individual gifts, which when fully used benefit the whole. Shaping ourselves to be *like* one another removes our propensity to be different or to celebrate differences.

We've forgotten something, I am sure. But it will be up to our children to take our new messages, which hopefully will be old to them, and in that distant port after we've been lost at sea, they will build a new ship with messages of their own, and repeat this old, old ritual of becoming truer to ourselves.

Paradox is the flower of the truth.

—Anonymous

The Shadow

We have met the enemy, and he is us.

—Walt Kelly

Here's a secret. There is only one person between you and a meaning-ful, fulfilling life. That's you. When you finally see what's been holding you back all these years, you will discover not an enemy, but yourself. A scared little Good Girl who was afraid of being different.

When you wait for other people to make life happen for you, it won't. Ever. Because your life requires you. It requires you to speak out, to listen, to act—all for the benefit of your dreams and needs.

When Olivia was asking, then screaming, nobody was listening because she was screaming at herself. Somehow, like many of the rest of us, she had forgotten herself. She took all the Good Girl messages to heart and was the house expert Pleaser, Performer, and Perfectionist. In taking on the roles she thought gained her approval and love, she stuffed down all the parts that weren't acceptable. She thought the power to live the life she wanted came from outside herself. Nobody listened, unless she screamed, because she wasn't listening to herself. And once she screamed, she created Performers and Pleasers, but not authenticity. Once she began to hear her-self and to believe she had the right to want something different, some-thing she could give to herself, she began to act upon it. And life began to transform…for her and for her family.

Our shadow may contain the best of ourselves.

—Marion Woodman

While Meg Murray realized *like* and *equal* are not the same, she still needed to remember the one thing she has that IT does not. As she was trying to remember, she thought about herself and Charles Wallace. "I love you even when I'm mad at you. I love you when others make fun of me because of you. I know what you like to eat. I know how to comfort and care for you. I love you no matter what others say or what you do." She figured it out. She had love. Unconditional love. She loved Charles Wallace, all the parts that bonded them as well as all the parts the other kids made fun of.

I was too wrapped up in wanting her (my daughter) to be perfect. But that's all about wanting yourself to look perfect. You know, not so much her grades, but manners and morals. I was very conscious of her doing the 'right' thing. Writing her thank you notes and being in the right places. I was raised that way, and it was all I knew.

And, I should have allowed a little more freedom there. I didn't know any different. But, she rebelled on some things that I never questioned. I was a people pleaser, and she was more of an independent thinker. And so we come to the road there and butt heads. You know you want your child to be a reflection of you, or rather you feel that way. I didn't put pressure on her so much as I did myself.

—Olivia, 65 years old

Unconditional love begins with us. We are bright, and we learned our lessons well. Only thing is the lessons are for a world that no longer exists, and can't instruct us on the world we want to build. The first thing we must do is go back for those parts we imprisoned, our Shadow Self. We must show the courage and fortitude to confront the IT of cultural messages and customs that Meg used in rescuing her brother. We must remember *equal* honors differences—of abilities, desires, and personality. And when we bring the hidden parts of ourselves to the light, we can once again be whole, as can our children, spouses, parents, and friends. Different, equal and whole.

Confront the dark parts of yourself, and work to banish them with illumination and forgiveness. Your willingness to wrestle with your demons will cause your angels to sing. Use the pain as fuel, as a reminder of your strength.

—August Wilson

CHAPTER TEN

Queens Want... What?

Love's Baptism

I'm ceded, I've stopped being theirs;
The name they dropped upon my face
With water, in the country church,
Is finished using now,
And they can put it with my dolls,
My childhood, and the string of spools
I've finished threading too.

Baptized before without the choice,
But this time consciously, of grace
Unto supremest name,
Called to my full, the crescent dropped,
Existence's whole arc filled up
With one small diadem.

My second rank, too small the first,
Crowned, crowing on my father's breast,
A half unconscious queen;
But this time, adequate, erect,
With will to choose or to reject
And I choose—just a throne.

—Emily Dickinson

MILY DICKINSON'S POEM of self-realization speaks of our introduction to the authority and culture that names us, but cannot claim us. A baby girl, crowing, unaware except of the love that supports her, is baptized on her father's breast, so near his heart, in his name. The infant has no choice in name—it will be her father's, or the ritual, his, too—which will be bestowed upon her. She is a half unconscious Queen.

But the child's consciousness cannot be contained by the constraint of authority, however loving, which is not hers. She might not fit the mold of domesticity, characterized by dolls and needlework. This child is not a princess to prick her finger on a spindle.

She is no longer 'theirs.' Born of them, she cannot belong to her parents or the past. When her consciousness, by Grace, is called to its fullest, the rank she was born to has become too small. Now as an adult, adequate in her own right, erect, not an infant in her father's arms, she chooses her second rank.

What has caused this change? Simply the Will to choose—or reject. In her original poem, unedited by her friends, Dickinson says she chooses— not a throne—but a crown. And the woman chooses a crown. She chooses to become her own authority. She has become a Queen.

We must always see we have choices. And we must find ones that will bring us closer to what we want.

—Susan O'Halloran and Susan Delattre

111

Excerpted from My Journal

I'm not sure what my problem is. I have so much, but still feel out of sorts. It's hard to label it, but even harder to figure out how to fix it. I go through the motions every day. I get up, go to work, come home and then go to bed. Oh, it's not all that bad. I have friends. I do laugh. I have fun. But, I'm missing something. What?

The Yellow Brick Road

"Ding, dong the witch is dead!" Let's look at the *Wizard of Oz* from the transformational aspect that we are all parts of our world. Dorothy, the Little Girl from Kansas, wanted to be good, but somehow her unruly little dog Toto constantly broke the rules. She chased after him; then found herself in so much trouble, she felt she must run away from home in order to save him. She tried, but her aunt's love called her back, only for her and Toto to be whisked off in a tornado and crashed in a far, fantastic country. The crash killed the Wicked Witch of the East, making a mortal enemy of her sister, The Wicked Witch of the West. To save herself and Toto this time, to find her way home, Dorothy had to accept the shoes of the dead witch, the blessings of Glinda, the Good Witch of the North. She had to set out on the Yellow Brick Road to seek help from the Great and Powerful Wizard of Oz. She was in a foreign land, where none of the rules she learned at home applied. Except for Toto, she began her journey alone.

But Dorothy and Toto didn't complete the trip by themselves…one by one she met three companions—the Scarecrow, the Cowardly Lion, and the Tin Woodsman—each feeling they were missing something as much as she missed home.

They did arrive in Oz, but the Wizard refused to give them what they wanted—passage home, a brain, courage and a heart, unless they accomplished another mission. Having freed Oz from the Wicked Witch of the East was not enough. She had to now free it from the Wicked Witch of the West. Instead of completing her mission she was captured by the evil Witch and her flying monkeys, and imprisoned in the castle.

Now it was Toto's turn to save her. He escaped and went back for her companions. But there was no end to wickedness. The witch set fire to the Scarecrow. Dorothy did the only thing reasonable. She picked up a bucket of water and threw it on him. Water happened to be the *only* substance that would destroy the evil Witch.

So, without forethought or pre-meditated plan, Dorothy prevailed over tyranny. She and her friends, freed, accomplished their task, and were entitled to receive their bequest from the Wizard.

Not so.

Turns out the Wizard was merely a cowardly little man filled with self-importance and misinformation who had himself wandered into Oz by mistake. The 'gifts' he gave to Dorothy's companions were merely symbols identifying qualities they already had. He invited Dorothy to fly off with him in his hot air balloon, and she accepted. Toto, as dear to her as her own heart and as unruly as ever, jumped from the balloon. Dorothy had to follow her beloved pup, even when it looked like he was heading in the wrong direction, even when authority told her to go another way, even if it meant she would never reach home again.

Thank goodness Toto sensed danger and jumped from the balloon, because traveling with the Wizard was unerringly wrong for Dorothy. The action of her roguish Toto, which appeared to be a dead end, was anything but. This dead end was actually the beginning—the beginning of Dorothy's emerging self, housing all those attributes she sought throughout her dream journey—courage, a heart and intellect. Her love led her to the *right* path to take her home.

What would have happened if Toto hadn't jumped? Dorothy's choice to trust the Wizard and take his path would have meant she was choosing to follow someone else's course, not her own—to take the longer and bumpier road. Continuing our imaginary story, Dorothy would have landed farther away from home—in another strange country with foreign customs, filled with detours and darkness. Scarecrow, Tin Woodman and Lion would have pursued her. They actually represented the qualities we are all born with—courage, love, and intellect—and though we may think we have left them behind, we cannot. These parts merely wait for us to use them. Imagine Dorothy waking up from her long journey some twenty-five to thirty years later. Still able to reach the final destination, the merging of all those parts—courage, love and intellect—Dorothy would eventually realize her own wholeness. She would have come home.

During her years with the Wizard, Dorothy would also not have been able to hear the true counsel of her inner wisdom, The Good Witch Glinda. The wrong choice didn't close the door to Glinda's guidance. Listening to the wrong counsel, the Wizard, Dorothy simply wouldn't be able to hear Glinda's message. Dorothy, relying on the opinion of others, had decided the Wizard was her only hope. Dorothy would have ignored her inner knowing and allowed herself to be influenced by outward appearances, thereby accepting an indirect route to her destination—home, herself, who she was born to be.

In the original story of *The Wizard of Oz*, Dorothy's magic shoes were silver. Symbolically, the color silver represents 'protective energy.' Throughout the story, her shoes remain Dorothy's protective energy. No matter how dangerous things seemed, she was protected as long as she wore the shoes.

Your journey, whether on course or off, will lead you home. You will be protected, and only given what is in your power to endure. The gift is to understand at any moment you can take the direct path to your next destination point. You can go directly there by listening to your inner guide and wisdom.

"You have always had the power to go home," Glinda told Dorothy after Toto led her out of the Wizard's balloon. "Close your eyes, tap your heels together and think to yourself, 'There's no place like home. There's no place like home.'"

Have you recognized how each of the players in *The Wizard of Oz* represents some aspect of the Hero's journey? Dorothy is the Good Little Girl who wants to fit the cultural patterns. Toto represents the part of her nature that doesn't conform to rules. As a result, he continually gets into trouble threatening his very existence. To protect him, Dorothy wants to run away, but the need for belonging to her family, to those who have cared for her, calls her to come back no matter what the price—even if the price is Toto. The tornado must come, and will come, as it comes to us all—the uncontrollable situation that will leave us stranded far from the familiar. The dead witch represents those cultural bindings that are the first casualty when we leave the fold, but we are far from healed.

With the blessings of our inner guide, the Good Witch Glinda, and silver slippers keeping us safe throughout our wanderings, we set out to seek the advice of the Authority. We think we are traveling alone, not knowing the companions who will keep us company. But courage, love, and intellect go with us. We won't know that until we use them.

When we act with great love, we overcome the dictates of cruel cultural authority, but we have a kinder, less obvious block to face—the dictates of an authority we want to obey, that we think will save us. And still our heart, like little Toto, won't let us rest. Listening to our own inner imperatives, we realize no one can save us. We are saved. We've always been saved. It's as simple as personal choice. And just like Dorothy. Click. Click. Click. We're home.

We must all recognize we have great love, great courage and great intellect for our own journey to wholeness. We must integrate them so the foghorn of other people's directions will mute, and we can hear our inner voice.

Just like Dorothy's Scarecrow, Tin Woodsman and Lion, we have always had what we needed to be whole. We allowed other influences—authority, culture and others' opinions—to direct us toward paths that aren't our own.

Unable to let go of our innate originality that gets us in trouble with the Powers That Tell Us How To Be, we feel we are carried far from home. Feeling lost, we follow the Yellow Brick Road while traipsing off to find a new authority, the Wizard, the Wonderful Wizard of Oz. We give our hopes and dreams to the all-powerful Wizard in the belief he can make us whole. Oh, he will give us tasks, all right, tasks that benefit lots of people. But make us whole? The all-powerful Oz can't. His authority is a sham— unworthy, unfair and full of fear. *He* is the outside influence. *He* is culture.

Simply put, any path you take isn't necessarily the wrong way to go. The indirect path merely takes you off course and makes the journey longer. Instead of developing our talents and interests full force at age twenty, most of us don't hit our peak until forty, fifty or sixty something. Most of us, for lack of knowledge, take the wrong path until we simply can go no further.

Tunnel Vision

My thresholds all seem to come by accident. See, I didn't make choices, my life just happened.

—Donna, 55 years old

Only she, who says she did not choose, is the loser in the end.

—Adrienne Rich

In *Invisible Acts of Power*, Caroline Myss says, "One day an image of the Yellow Brick Road from the film *The Wizard of Oz* snapped into my mind, and I saw that each of us is meant to follow a particular path that reveals itself to us. We are meant to treat our life as a journey, and at each step on that journey, we are meant to notice what is around us and act on opportunities that present themselves.

How we act—the decisions and choices we make when we face opportunities or challenges—helps us develop inner strength. This is how we become empowered human beings."

As a young adult, I found myself at the crossroad many, many times. I typically didn't make good choices. I couldn't hear my inner guidance/ heart, my Good Witch Glinda. External directives muddled her voice. Trying very hard to please everyone but myself, I blocked the messages softly calling from my heart.

There were many times I didn't make a choice at all. I figured if I stood there long enough, the choice would go away. Usually it did, but I discovered the old adage to be true…not making a choice *is* a choice. Each time fear paralyzed me I felt I had lost ground, gone backwards. Recall the analogy of painting yourself into a corner. Once there, you have no way out—at least not until all the paint dries.

Take the riskiest path you can find—it's an illusion. The safe path is the *real* illusion.

—Caroline Myss

Security is mostly a superstition. It does not exist in nature.

—Helen Keller

Many people attempt to make decisions based on factors of safety: finances, shelter, love. Selecting what is perceived as the 'safe' choice might be remaining where you are when, in fact, that very well might be the most dangerous choice you could make. Without the universal view, your understanding of what's in front of you will most likely be distorted. Remember Dorothy's hot air balloon ride? If your guides are external to yourself—culture, other people, authority figures, or fears—you've got a fifty-fifty chance that the choice you make will be the right one for the moment, but it will never be the right one for you, because you will never believe in yourself. If other people decide what's right for you, you will never experience your own validity. You will always feel wrong, no matter how favorable the immediate situation resolves.

The Rank Too Small

If a girl doesn't have her husband's name, then she has her father's name. How fair is that?

—Lauren Gray, *Judging Amy*

It was like having tunnel vision growing up. There were no forks in the road.

—Diane, 56 years old

Many of the women who shared their voices with me did not feel aware of actually having a choice they elected for themselves. Most shared a 'tunnel vision' perspective, admitting that early in their adult lives they didn't have enough information to make more appropriate choices. Particularly women over fifty didn't see many options.

Some bought into the cultural messages about what a woman could and couldn't do at home and at work. Others believed being a mother, wife and daughter would always be enough. A fifty-six-year-old Mississippi Delta woman said, "I think it was because I always thought I would not have any choices. Everything was decided for me. That belief came from being a girl growing up and that you did what you were told, and no questions asked."

Another fifty-something-year-old woman shared, "It's just something I never really thought about. I had to do it and I was expected to do what I was told. You know, you minded your mother and father. Someone always directed you. You got married and it was the husband calling the shots. I never saw any choice as being my own." A fifty-four-year-old subject claimed, "When I was growing up I didn't think I had any choices."

Many of the women I interviewed shared their feelings of pain at being unable to get their needs met. Some of them felt if they had believed they had options when they were younger, they would indeed be Queens—happy Queens, at that. But some of the women taking the path of least resistance, the familiar path laid out by cultural dictates, discovered the reality of being a Queen never transpired. Instead they followed the rules, played the game as instructed and wound up with a life filled with frustrations, anger and unhappiness.

I didn't know about all the choices. I did some interviews for a women's studies class—it was a generational paper. I interviewed my mother. I can remember thinking, "Is my mother satisfied with her life?"

—Kathy, 35 years old

Like so many women of her generation, she had graduated directly from her mother's extended household to her own nuclear family, and had no experience of living alone. So, one morning, she simply woke up knowing in her bones that this life that she had not so much chosen, but fallen into nearly two decades ago, was no longer—if it ever was—good for her.

—Donna Henes

If Not This—Then, What?

In my first foray into the career world, I secured a coveted internship, which when completed, would grant me entrance into a competitive clinical psychology graduate program. I knew I wasn't happy with my career choice. I wasn't cut out to be a scientist/psychologist, but I think I would have made a wonderful counselor. Listening to my authority figures—those learned doctors—I ignored my Good Witch Glinda.

After I realized I did not want a future in the clinical psychology option, I felt directionless, lost. I had to find a new goal. My college roommate, Jill, proceeded directly to banking. She excelled in her environment while surrounding herself with young, passionate business wannabes. I think it was Jill's success and comfort that initially pulled me into the world of money and finance. As a result, I ended up with a minor in the field. The business school felt familiar and safe.

It didn't hurt that my father, a businessman, posted a newspaper ad about a local college's MBA program on the fridge. I walked by it daily, noticing it almost at every turn.

Over a two-month period, the idea grew on me. I had been successful in undergraduate business courses. An MBA graduate could do just about anything in business. Wherever my Greg's path took him would include a university with a business graduate school. The summer after our wedding, I made my announcement. "I'm going to get an MBA!"

I had found a practical, doable and successful route, a career choice that would ensure my ability to support myself and others. I hit it with the same enthusiasm I had my 'psychology career.'

I was relieved I had a direction again and could march onward—onward to something that actually took me farther off course at the time. During my post-MBA years, I took one unfulfilling job after another—never finding my place.

As far as finding my prince and starting a family went, from early adolescence, I had realized I didn't like my 'womanly' choices. To me, being a female seemed unfair. I didn't want to do all the 'duties' required by virtue of my gender. My personal version of tunnel vision helped me concoct a completely inappropriate fairy tale vision of marriage. I was to be a full-time professional Queen with hired help—a housecleaner, nanny and cook.

Of course, my reality didn't shape up that way. I ended up marrying my high school sweetheart, so our journey together started from the beginning of our careers. We didn't make enough money for me to live my fantasy life. I worked full-time, cared for my daughter and held all the domestic responsibilities, too.

If you recall, that is where I crashed and burned. I couldn't keep up the pace. For survival purposes, I had to stop.

As I experienced the transition, I shocked myself. How did I have the courage to go through with it? Besides breaking a promise to the man that hired me, I also was giving up a hefty paycheck and benefits. That breakthrough was a turning point for me. Finally, I was ready to play a different game. With my shortsightedness removed, I could create a plan that allowed me to follow my heart.

My ability to finally see clearly resulted from my personal experience. I had the ability to see what I *didn't* want, to set goals, and to achieve them. But still I was heartsick. How can your goals satisfy you when their purpose is to take you away from what you *don't* want? Goals are needed to achieve what you do want.

My transition began with asking the right questions: Why wasn't I happy? What would make me happy? By asking the right questions, I had already begun to make new choices appropriate for my unique course through life.

Now this may sound reversed, but I had begun living my new path when I started interviewing women for the Gender Project (this book). Talking with other women clarified it for me. I had begun living my life, but the experience of other women helped me see the life I was living more clearly. Not surprisingly, I found so many women who sacrificed themselves to the family. But I also found women who felt family was their only course in life, and they were glad of it. My dialogues with a large number of women provided me a completely different and new perspective.

As I grew up, I made every effort to avoid women's work. I assumed all the women I knew felt the same way. Notice the key word in that last sentence, 'I.' If I hated it, then so did they. Right? *Wrong.*

I didn't really care about having a career. I loved being a homemaker. I loved being a wife. I don't feel less important. I feel my job in our family is just as important as my husband's.

—Kitty, 60 years old

Kitty thrived in her role as housewife and domestic leader. "I am incredibly comfortable in my skin. I know my heart."

Not until I matured did I realize how wrong I had been. It wasn't about the role women played, necessarily, it was how they *fit* the role. Some women relished the 'dolls and threads' Emily Dickinson's queen rejected.

It was a matter of knowing your heart. Graduating from high school, I knew only that I wasn't going to be a housewife. I had big plans—places to go, people to see, somebody to be. Not only would I have a career and 2.5 children, but also I would work at least forty hours outside the home and have someone else care for my children.

Turns out this fantasy didn't fit me, either. Believe me, I tried it. Because I was so far removed from my inner knowing at the time, I was even more shocked that once I jumped off my madness train, I was happier than I have ever been in my life. Oops! Suddenly, I was a stay-at-home mom with a low-key, part-time job and I loved my life.

It appeared I wasn't the only one confused by the mixed messages out there. A fifty-nine-year-old subject said, "I was drawn to women who were successful career women. And yet, I wanted to play bridge, sit with my friends by the pool or do the Junior League stuff. So, I always felt like an 'in between' person." The same subject continued, "I could have fought. I could have had the glass ceiling. But I chose what was comfortable. Right or wrong? I wasn't up to a fight. I never enjoyed confrontation. It was uncomfortable to me."

I balked at the feminist message I thought I heard—that women *shouldn't* like being caregivers for their families, that women *should* be relentless in the workplace, that women *should* be just like men, and cripple any man who thought differently. Only thing is I believed most of it, except maybe for the crippling part. I just didn't like how they said it. But it turned out I was right again, without knowing it. I didn't like the essential part of the message …you know, *should* and *shouldn't*.

Through this process of growing up, I learned something valuable. There is no Law of What You Are Supposed to Do. Each person, following her unruly heart, must decide what fits her. Okay, so should each man. One person might fit a cultural pattern exactly; another will not. It's not a certain choice that's right or wrong, it's the *should* or *should not* that creates the confusion, roadblocks and pain.

Interestingly, of all the women I interviewed the women who neither married nor had children appeared to be the most fulfilled in their respective roles later in life. Why should this be? Perhaps because they questioned the cultural dictates early in their lives, and felt they could choose their own way without sacrificing themselves or the people they were supposed to care for. By not becoming wives and mothers, they were not bound by tradition, and they felt free to become more fully themselves.

I don't believe every woman should be a wife or a mother. At the same time, for those of us who have a deep longing for the connectiveness of family, there needs to be a better way. Our commitments to each other should not result in losing ourselves.

That's why looking at the entrenched lessons handed down by the Monarchy, reinforced by conditional love and further refined by Southern Rules, we may see clearly enough to know the answer to the right questions. If we are not happy, it may be that other people's answers don't fit our world; instead of us being so wrong, we don't fit the world we were born into.

One of my favorite scenes in the movie *Fried Green Tomatoes* is when two young, spunky girls whip into the parking space Evelyn Couch is trying to maneuver into.

"Just face it lady, we're younger and faster than you are," one of them tells her. They both laugh.

Evelyn comes to the end of her 'be nice' rope. She only takes a moment to consider before she begins ramming their red beetle car with her own sedan. "Ladies, let's face it," she tells the now screaming duo. "I'm older and have more insurance than you do."

Evelyn, after a lifetime of compliance and sacrifice, is waking up. She is tired of the rules that seem to demand she 'be nice' while giving nothing in return. Being older and having insurance are symbols of the experience and ability to take care of herself. She is learning to choose and decide for herself. She has seceded. She is no longer 'Theirs'—those Southern Rules (or her sub-cultural messages) that bound her to fit their shape.

The scene is funny to those of us who believed in the cultural rules that had entrapped Evelyn most of her life. But if Evelyn had realized her own resources earlier, she could have bypassed the frustration and rage it took to wake her up.

Eventually, I learned it was not my job to shelve my dreams in the support of others. It was not okay to accept life as other people decried it should be. With new insight, I realized that I wanted to teach my daughter she had been born with a great power. She had been born with the power of choice.

CHAPTER ELEVEN

The Queen's Heart

Now We Know to Choose, What Are We Choosing For?

In the lives of many people it is possible to find a unifying purpose that justifies the things they do day in, day out—a goal that like a magnetic field attracts their psychic energy, a goal upon which all lesser goals depend…Without such a purpose, even the best-ordered consciousness lacks meaning.

—Mihaly Csikszentmihalyi

HE SORROW AND confusion I've felt all of my life often puzzled me. I had kind and loving parents who believed in me. I was given everything I needed, and an abundance of what I wanted. I had been amply educated. I had a loving husband. While I might not have liked many of my jobs, I was eminently employable. I was able to focus and meet goals. While money was often tight in the beginning, my husband and I were able to make ends meet and still have some fun stuff in our lives. I've heard F. Scott Fitzgerald once said, "It's hard to feel sorry for a boy on a boat." Of course, the boy would have been a millionaire, and the

124

boat, a yacht. But during those years I felt so sad, lost, and well, rudderless, I often felt like that girl on that boat...my life really wasn't terrible, so *I* must be.

That statement is absolutely right. No, my life wasn't so terrible. I must Be.

Deepak Chopra in his *Seven Laws of Spiritual Success,* talks about the Law of Dharma. Dharma simply means purpose in life. He says each of us is here to discover our true Self by expressing our unique talents to serve humanity.

That's not so far from the Rules of Monarchy, which teach women should express their talents to serve the King and the Royal Family and all the friends, family, and organizations she encounters. For this she will receive approval and love. And quite possibly she feels without approval and love, she will not belong to the Kingdom, and she will die condemned, shunned, alone.

It's not quite the same. Polly Berrien Berends, author of *Whole Child, Whole Parent,* says we are born whole, and the job of parents is not to mold the child, but to let her true nature unfold. Just as we are born with the physical genes for the color of our skin, curly hair or straight, freckles or not, we are born with innate talents. If we trace our interests and desires, we can find evidence of them from earliest childhood.

Often it is those innate talents, driven by dreams and curiosity, which make us *different,* which get us into as much trouble as Dorothy's little Toto found with the hateful neighbor, Miss Gulch. If we come into this world whole, and are unfolding to our true purpose, then often applying the Rules of the Kingdom, which are designed to make us *alike,* to win approval from others, are akin to someone 'helping' a rose to bloom 'better' by pulling apart its petals to wrest them into a more pleasing shape.

You are unique, and if that is not fulfilled, something has been lost.

—Martha Graham

Doing and Being Are Not the Same

"What do you fear my lady?"
"A cage. To stay behind bars until use and old age accept them, and all chance of valor has gone beyond recall or desire."

—Arwen, *Lord of the Rings: The Twin Towers*

My mother started telling me when I was little…Don't let anyone cause you to try to be somebody else.

—Christine, 91 years old

Berends speaks of how hard it was to help her little boy separate his worth from his doings. "Um," she would say when he brought her cookies he had just baked. "These are really, really good."

"I'm a good boy, aren't I?" he would ask, identifying with the success of his task.

She wanted him to know his worth was not dependent on how good his cookies were. "You *are* a good boy," she would say, "and these are really good *cookies*."

If we equate worth with what we do, we are placing ourselves in a cage, creating a new Authority with rigid rules about how we must please… even if the tyrant we are pleasing is ourselves. We become our actions. We become someone else.

Man's ideal state is realized when he has fulfilled the purpose for which he is born. And what is it that reason demands of him? Something very easy—that he lives in accordance with his own nature.

—Seneca

So, what is this concept called purpose? Finding purpose means finding something bigger than yourself. There's more to it than that, though. Quite possibly feeling pushed towards something bigger, you must find what brings you a sense of fulfillment—feelings like peace and joy.

Notwithstanding, you must reach this place while also living comfortably in the present.

Impossible? I don't think so. I think it is highly feasible to live in a purposeful state. For over a decade, I looked for the *perfect* job to supply me with purpose. I had a warped notion that purpose was tied to occupation. Hang on to that idea and you will experience pain. Save yourself the trouble and start believing that purpose has nothing to do with your vocation. Purpose is about self-awareness and development. It's tuning in to a bigger picture—God's perspective—while altering your approach to life.

Be the change you want to see in the world.

—Mahatma Gandhi

It's about practicing forgiveness, truthfulness, love and kindness. It's about being the best person you can be despite your situation or circumstances. It's about moving forward without regret while being willing to let go of fear-based thinking. Living on purpose means you remove fear from your bag of tricks. With a much lighter bag to drag around, you start listening to yourself—your heart starts to sing, and you hear it. Finally removing all the clutter, you will know what to do. Your new life will be structured around the essence of what you desire—not your career. You will find your Self. And then, as Deepak Chopra stated, by using your unique talents, you will find yourself serving humanity. And loving it.

Philosophical ponderings about purpose and meaning are all well and good, but how do you conjure up contentment? As I muddled through my own search, I discovered it was much more important to recognize your talents than to use them in a way that felt insignificant. Countless numbers of people already know they are in the wrong place, but many times being in the wrong place means being surrounded by negative, angry people; working in a position that emphasizes your weaknesses or downplays your talents; or facing circumstances that continually question your moral or ethical beliefs. For example, traditional employment always violated my need for freedom and rarely did I find a flexible structure within a corporate or business system. By recognizing that there is a problem, you are compelled to seek out change. Once understanding that the environment is toxic, you must correct it, or it will be corrected for you.

Recently, I received an email from an old friend in Texas explaining how she suddenly found herself fired. The story led into a request for me to write a résumé. In her opinion, she was the victim. In my detached view, she created a firing. "My boss said I had no project management skills, and I brought my personal problems to work. Now I really do need to find a new job!" She continued her saga by saying, "I have not been happy at that job for a very long time. Now, I have a reason to look for a new one." Her unhappiness had been going on for three years. Enough already.

For some reason, we have bought into the belief that there is nothing else as good as what we have. This is it. If I move or change, I will be worse off than I was before.

Use Everything

You were born with potential.
You were born with goodness and trust.
You were born with ideals and dreams.
You were born with greatness.
You were born with wings.
You are not meant to crawl, so don't.
You have wings.
Learn to use them and fly.

—Rumi

If you are unhappy with any part of your life situation, know you are not fulfilling your purpose. You are living in a cage. You are living someone else's life. Your unhappiness is a gift. Listen. It is your Unlived Life calling to you.

Now here is a secret. When you have done the work, listened to your Shadow Self, rediscovered your innate talents, changed the course of your life, do not think you will live happily ever after. Life that does not grow withers. The time will come when your new home becomes a cage, your new self will have expended herself. And from within, you will hear the call.

Heed it. Don't make what worked yesterday today's Authority.

Georgia Richardson (a.k.a. Queen Jaw Jaw) shared with me her life's purpose. Borrowing from Erma Bombeck she said, "When I stand before God at the end of my life, I would hope that I would not have a single bit of talent left, and could say: I used everything you gave me."

Using all your talent today may mean changes in your life's path. Over and over the time will come when you must choose or regret. Choosing is the door that opens to invite your purpose in. The will to choose is what makes a Queen.

It is good to have an end to journey towards; but it is the journey that matters, in the end.

—Ursula K. LeGuin

CHAPTER TWELVE

Changing the Guard

Women have to come to understand ourselves as central, not peripheral, before anything real can happen. We have to depend on our ourselves…This cannot be done against men…It cannot be woman against man. It has to be woman finding her true self with or without man, but not against man.

—May Sarton

WE WERE BORN in our father's house, given his name, given his customs. Those customs told us our worth and being depended on fitting ourselves to the customs. We came to see ourselves as peripheral. What we wanted, what we cared about personally, was minor, and easily eclipsed, sometimes deeply buried. Our goodness depended on what other people thought of us, so we tried really hard to be good. We pricked our finger on the spindle of the culture we were born into. We fell asleep. In our dreaming we climbed into the Wizard's hot air balloon and traveled to his country, not ours. But we're waking up. We don't want to travel under the Wizard's guidance anymore. We were born whole, and we want to claim that wholeness.

So, what do we do now?

First, we have to understand we were born with a unique purpose. As May Sarton says, we have to come to understand we are central to our lives. We are not defined by authority or by culture. Neither, do we need to fight against the powers that be. This also means it is no longer necessary to kow-tow to them either. We must turn our attention to our own sources of pain and to our own dreams.

They will provide us with a map, to point us toward our unique purpose, the one unfolding in our life. But first, we must begin the process of understanding ourselves as central. First, we must forgive the past—others for hurting us, and ourselves for being hurt. And we must face our worst enemy, the enemy who, no matter how good things might be, no matter how hard we try to make things better, no matter how much the world offers us its abundance, will tell us in very mean ways we are fakes, losers, and are no good. We must face ourselves.

It's So Hard to Change, I Get So Tired, Why Keep Trying?

Most people prefer the certainty of misery to the misery of uncertainty.

—Virginia Satir

Before we get started trying to make things different, perhaps we should look at why we are stuck where we are. Behavior repeats itself when there is a pay-off. What is the pay-off for negative self-talk? Simple. We do not have to be the Authority in our own lives. Somehow, we have internalized the message we are less than, that other people dictate our lives, that our choices for ourselves must meet with everyone else's approval. In essence, we are keeping life the way it's always been.

But what if suddenly we realized we not only can create the life we want, but we've created the life we have. Could we endure the guilt? And we have no maps. How could we be different? Rather than *bad*, we'd be *nothing*. Not true.

What you will have done is open all the doors you closed on what you thought was the unacceptable parts of yourself. When you forgive, when you stop beating yourself up with mean thoughts, your Unlived Life can emerge. Your Shadow Self can introduce herself. You can choose instead of regret. You've become the adult.

But as I explained in the beginning of this email, my foot hurts, the heel, that is. I have been to see the osteopath, but a closer look at Lise Bourbeau's book tells me that this may be because I can't seem to move forward as I would—that I only do things when I have the consent of those around me.

—Gena, 47 years old

As long as Dorothy is wearing her silver slippers, she is protected. Not even the Wicked Witch of the West can hurt her. Why? For the same reason the shoes can take her home. Those shoes, those symbolic shoes, represent her two good feet, which can take her anywhere she wishes to go. They represent consent…her own for herself. Yes, we buried those 'unacceptable' parts of ourselves so many years ago. We have kept them hidden under the tyranny of fear and guilt, and just plain meanness. When they begin to emerge, we will be terrified. But let them come. You are protected. You have your own consent for your own life to be lived. You have the power of choice. By your will, you are Queen.

Take your life in your own hands, and what happens? A terrible thing: no one to blame.

—Erica Jong

Forgiveness

In fact, not forgiving is like drinking rat poison and then waiting for the rat to die.

—Anne Lamott

None of us escapes life unscathed. We have been raised under the rules of the Monarchy, and further cinched in by local customs. We feel loved only when we are performing well. Everyone. No one escapes the process. And we pass the pain we've accumulated on to one another, in the guise of rules of our own, as a way to steal power when we feel powerless. This means we have been hurt, and we have hurt others. It means we have turned our attention away from ourselves and toward the ones we feel inflicted this pain.

We can't find ourselves when we're pointing at others. I know some of us have experienced horrific conditions and have come away with serious wounds. But if we remain trapped in the past, we bring the past with us. It will poison our present and stunt our future. Our purpose is not based on receiving retribution or revenge. The truth is, nobody can change the past. But the past can only intrude on the present if we bring it with us as a burden weighing us down.

Many of us refuse to forgive because we want to protect ourselves. We may think forgiveness is in our best interest. We may want to forgive, we may say we forgive, but let us think of the old wound, and it feels immediate and deadly. It hurts right now, and we didn't want to be hurt anymore.

How do we heal the wounds inflicted so long ago?

Many times I went through the motions of asking for forgiveness. Initially, I did little things like trying to send those I disliked positive thoughts. I never confronted any of my offenders face-to-face. Instead, I whispered that I forgave them for all their transgressions. Then I released them from my thoughts, so I believed.

The only problem with going through the motions of forgiveness is that you also must feel it. There were some folks I tried to forgive, but in their presence, I still felt damaged, hurt or mad. When that occurs, I know it's time once again to make my forgiveness official.

The process takes time—like any transformation. In my case, forgiveness did not immediately happen. All in all, I've probably gone through the motions of forgiving some three to five times in my life.

My forgiveness practice begins with writing down the names of all the people I can think of I need to forgive. As I think of each person, I forgive her or him, as well as myself, for the past. I ask to be released from the pain. I consider it done.

Fortune cookies, postcards, bumper stickers, everything but sky writing—yet I kept feeling that I could not, would not forgive her in a box, could not would not forgive with a fox, not on a train, not in the rain.

—Anne Lamott

When this process is begun, many people find the ones they are forgiving, especially those who still caused them stress or pain, show back up in their life. This happened to me.

Following the completion of my MBA degree, I temporarily worked for a consultant I admired. I wanted to be exactly what she was. I was thrilled she decided to take me on and show me the ropes. We agreed she'd pay me a minimum retainer, with a commission or payment for other work I performed. The relationship lasted three months. What a disaster.

She asked me to leave. Yep, consider myself fired. I left with my tail tucked. The experience was a major disappointment and setback. The time with Marianne—no, that's not her real name—altered my path and left me floundering. Before the final break in our working relationship, I dreamed about her. She was wearing a brightly colored, *very* gaudy clown outfit—complete with the hat and red nose. She was laughing boisterously, making quite a scene. Thinking back on it now makes me smile because my inner guide—my smart Good Witch Glinda—knew (I'm sure from the very beginning) that Marianne was not at all what she appeared to be.

The clown analogy was perfect. Everything about her was an exaggeration. When I looked at Marianne without listening to my intuition, I saw a kind, intelligent mentor doing something that I thought I wanted to do—a protective mother figure, someone who embraced me warmly. When my inner guide looked at her, she saw a woman not yet emotionally mature enough to mentor another person. The experience confused me.

Forgiving Marianne was difficult. Returning from a family visit, I waited in the baggage claim area for my husband to pick me up. Over the intercom I heard, "Marianne Smith, Marianne Smith, please pick up a pager phone." I cringed and quickly exited the building. More than five years after the firing, I still wasn't able to handle a face-to-face interaction. She was *always* on my forgiveness list, and I simply couldn't make it real. No matter how hard I tried, it wasn't happening.

It took many times for me to really mean it—to know that if I saw her, I would be okay and no longer tied to an emotional response. When I finally did forgive her, she seemed to know it. A couple of weeks after the 'forgiveness' ceremony, I got a call from Marianne's assistant. Marianne, now a vice president of a local company, wanted to know if I needed a job.

Although since the firing, I've never had to endure a face-to-face meeting with her, I would be comfortable seeing her again. The meeting would elicit no pain—I would not send daggers her way nor would I feel the need to do that anymore.

Forgiveness is never a one-way street. During my trial of forgiveness, I had to forgive myself for being vulnerable—for not being able to cope with Marianne and for being inexperienced enough to be hurt by her.

When we forgive, we change. Sometimes, I think we forget the other person changes, too.

The basic change that results from forgiveness is healing. When we can't forgive, we are saying we are the vulnerable, frightened person who suffered the original pain. We have not only brought our accusations from the past to the present, but we have also brought the wound. We see ourselves as we thought our tormentor saw us. When we finally are able to forgive, we have asked our Unlived Life, our Shadow Self to come into the light. We have remembered our silver slippers. We have become a new person. We have become whole.

There are many forgiveness practices. Find one that fits you. Remember your pain or hurt. Say hello to it. Speak about it. Then be willing to let it go. Do this each time the pain resurfaces. Each time you are willing to let it go, the bundled energy in the pain is released a bit more. One day you will find it is gone. You will find you are a different person. You have become a person who has chosen to choose rather than regret…you have chosen a crown. Indeed, you are a Queen.

Self Talk

We are back in junior high. So many adult women think they are stupid and ugly. Many feel guilty if they take time for themselves. Many do not express anger or ask for help.

—Mary Pipher

Remember Stanley Milgram and the Obedience to Authority experiments, the one where fake doctors got volunteer 'teachers' to shock fake 'learners' when the learners answered questions incorrectly? Self-talk is gatekeeper for the Authority of the Monarchy. No guards are needed. Given even a short period of time, we become the teachers, hawk-eyed keepers of the Way Things Ought to Be, eagerly punishing every transgression we might commit against the all-mighty Authority.

For many of us, we are back in junior high in an instant, incessantly hammering our own sins home with a barrage of mean talk. When I asked other women about their inner dialogue, nearly half of them reported negative messages. One woman said, "They are mixed. I think everything is, 'I have to, I should, I need to'. And, if I don't get it all done, then I think, 'What's wrong with me?' Actually, they are probably more negative than positive."

Another woman reported having a difficult childhood shared, "My messages are mostly negative. It goes back to hiding things. I don't think anyone realizes that you can keep how insecure you are so tightly wrapped up. People think I'm confident and outgoing. I also remember the messages from childhood, 'You are stupid. That's silly. That's ridiculous.' I still see myself like that. Once a counselor said to me, 'Why can you talk so wonderfully about others, but not about yourself?'"

A fifty-something female shared, "My inner dialogue has to do with being a perfectionist. I constantly say to myself: 'That could be better.' But, it helps me get it right."

My biggest hurdle in finding my own way in life was self-talk. My negative self-chatter was constant. *Fatty. Ugly. Stupid.* First, I had to realize what I was doing. Then I began monitoring myself. Slowly, over a period of about two years, I stopped the onslaught. Occasionally I slip, but now I've trained myself to immediately evaluate what I've said and why.

Most commonly I beat myself up about my appearance and my interactions with others. If I wasn't calling myself *Fatty*, I was slapping myself around with "Oh, I shouldn't have said that. Why are you so loud? That's not nice to say."

Sometimes I could distract myself over finances. You know, "How are we going to make it? I never should have bought that. We'll never be able to afford it." Following the good advice of motivational writer John Randolph Price, I replace worries and concerns with the statement: "God is my source, my substance and my supply." It works every time and immediately moves me away from worrying about something I can't fix at the moment.

Inner dialogue can cover a range of topics. Other common themes you might conjure up include:

The 'Woe Is Me' Dialogue

Many of us don't have everything we desire at the moment we desire it. That's because plenty of us haven't mastered our ability to co-create or manifest our dreams—success, money, security, peace, financial security, happiness. Constantly telling ourselves what we don't have or what we yearn for in our lives is not the road to riches.

Instead, use that inner chatterbox for good—create, plan and continually state your goals. When the negative messages start rolling in, redirect your thoughts. One quick start toward changing yourself talk and changing your life is to think of one action you *can* do toward obtaining the goal you do want. Implement that one action as soon as possible. Every time you realize you've slipped into 'woe-is-me' mode, think of your very doable step for the life you *do* want. Soon you will see where the power in your own life resides.

The 'Hanging on to the Past' Dialogue

The past is not always a nice place to hang out. You might have some pretty rough memories to tell the story. Thinking of the past allows you to dwell on revenge, anger, hurt—all the wrongs done you while preventing you from living in the present moment.

If you find the inner dialogue focused on your intent to pay back others, it's time to create new messages for yourself. Reviewing the past can be helpful. That's what I did while writing this book. However, the purpose for the review should focus on understanding and forgiveness—not, regret or revenge.

The 'If It Ain't Broke, Don't Fix It' Dialogue

If you continually respond to your situation by saying, "I hate my life, but I will just stay here and see what happens," it's time to change your message. I know a lady that is still slaving away at a job she has hated ever since I first met her—that was some twenty years ago. Her internal messages spoke often: "Where will I find a job as flexible as this one with the same pay? Who would hire me? There are no other jobs out there for me." Of course, there are plenty of other opportunities out there, but not if you don't think so.

My guess is that in another twenty years, she'll still be there. We were not put here to endure or live half-conscious lives. We were put here to learn, grow and be the brightest light possible. Thinking small, as well as limited, makes us small and limited. We weren't given dreams so that we would suffer more. We were given dreams so that we could transform ourselves…so that we can fulfill our purpose. Old, worn-out messages restricting our lives and happiness are just that—old and worn out. Replace the 'it's always been that way message' with a new line.

Ask the right question. What is it about this situation that makes me unhappy? Follow it with the next right question. What circumstances would make me happy? Be specific. And make sure the answers reflect what you want, not what you want someone else to do. Just being aware where your power resides is often enough to start making small changes in your life. And small changes are all that's needed to create the life you want.

The 'What Will They Think' Dialogue

Replaying the tape that reminds you that your neighbor's opinions are important is a dangerous game. Recently, I was talking to a friend who said, "Yes, mother thinks I should go to Rachel's party because I'm her friend. You know, she's having her annual big-bash and well, maybe I should go."

I responded, "Oh, is that when you'll be visiting?"

My friend replied, "No, I'd be making a special trip. Do you think I should go?"

My thoughts raced. "Let me get this straight. You live over 1,000 miles away from your friend. You aren't planning a trip. Claim to be in financial straits. Think you should buy a ticket for the 'big bash?' Why? Because your mother thinks it's a good idea to demonstrate your friend-ship? Did I miss something?" I wanted to say.

Another friend is all fired up about a new opportunity—moving to a new city and starting a new business. Even her husband is excited, but they hesitate because the grandparents will not approve. The grandparents have a perfect little world—all of their children and grandchildren live within fifteen minutes of their home. The choice for my friend—making a move that excites her and her husband, or staying put because it will upset the grandparents—is a tough one…for them.

The problem for these two dear people is that they cannot get beyond the "Momma and Daddy will not like it" mentality. From an outsider's point of view, they run all of their actions through the filter of their own parents' 'good opinion.' When your main concern is "what will they think of us," you cannot proceed to explore loving plans where everyone wins.

Of course we want to please our parents. Of course. But, we must stop pleasing them and others at the expense of exploring our own purpose and using our own talents. We owe our parents a lot, but not our lives. We don't owe anyone our lives. And that's one of the best lessons we can teach our children.

The 'Stop the Presses! The World Doesn't Revolve Around You' Dialogue.

Watching cartoons one day with my daughter, we happened to catch *Fairly Oddparents,* a story about little Timmy Turner and his two fairy godparents. On this episode, Timmy is granted the ability to read the minds of others. At one point after correctly answering an oral quiz, he thinks, "I bet my classmates are thinking I'm wonderful!" He turns to one and hears, "This growth has a life of its own. Oh, I hope no one has noticed." He then turns to another and picks up, "I should have known the answer. I am stupid. Stupid. Stupid." Still looking to stroke his own ego, he picks another target only to hear something like: "They all must hate me! What is wrong with me?"

Another great lesson for children is to help them understand that the world does *not* revolve around them. Rarely is another individual focused on you, re-hashing your voice tone, your choice of words, your lack of intelligence over and over in their minds. If you could read other people's minds, you would have a revelation similar to Timmy's. His supposedly brilliant answer was not even noted by any of his classmates. Instead he discovered all his friends obsessing about themselves.

I once worked with a woman who constantly doubted herself—clearly beating herself up emotionally almost on the minute. I know this because she often turned to outsiders to gather external confirmation of her continual failings. From my perspective, her self-hate was blown way out of proportion. Her interpretation of events was always negative and inaccurate. Her perceived missteps were only real in her imagination.

This woman was going through life saying, like Dorothy, "lions and tigers and bears, oh my." She never stopped to realize her companions, courage, heart and intellect, were with her all the time.

To stop the bombardment of damaging self-talk is not easy, but it's necessary. You want love and acceptance from your spouse, friends, colleagues or your parents, but you must give it to yourself first. If you don't, you simply will not recognize the goodness life sends your way.

How do you get started loving yourself? It's easier than you think.

When you notice those presses rolling, take deep breaths. Remember your silver slippers…that the power you were given at your birth is still with you, in you. And begin by being kind to yourself.

The 'Change It' Dialogue

Take a few days to monitor your self-talk. Jot down some of the nasty messages you share with yourself and record the intensity of the meanness. You might be in for a big shock. I know I was when I did this little exercise. I was awful to myself.

Continue to evaluate your words. With each offense, change the message until your inner talk is as friendly and gentle as if your best friend were talking to you. If your best friend is talking to you as mean as you have been talking to yourself, get a new best friend.

Eventually, you can alter your messages. It takes time and thought. During the time that you are monitoring your thoughts, start creating new messages to replace them. Instead of thinking: "Fat pig! You've got to lose weight," say, "I am losing weight easily and effortlessly."

If you are fussing at yourself about money, replace it with the message I mentioned from Mr. Price: "God is my source, my substance and my supply." What about the times when you talk about how stupid you are? Instead say something like: "I am divinely guided when I speak and communicate with others."

Another trick that works for me is using appreciation. Once you recognize the downward spiral, immediately respond by thinking of all the good in your life. "I love my big backyard. I have such wonderful friends who always cheer me up. I appreciate my children."

Whatever works for you is best. Make it simple. Make it elaborate. Make it work.

One author recommended wearing a rubber band around your wrist and snapping it every time you play the negative tape. Ouch! Personally, I stick to self-monitoring minus pain.

James Allen, author of *As A Man Thinketh*, wrote the book inspired by the Bible verse, "As a man thinketh, so he is." He claimed that it is within the power of each person to form his own character and create his own happiness based on his thoughts. Basically, a person is who she thinks she is. If she continues to think the same way, so she remains.

Stop Being Offended

Being offended is the natural consequence of leaving the house.

—Fran Lebowitz

I'm not offended by all the dumb blonde jokes because I know I'm not dumb…I also know I'm not blonde.

—Dolly Parton

As noted humorist Fran Lebowitz noted, running into other people's bad opinions is a condition of life. But Dolly Parton illustrates a crucial fact about those bad opinions. They can only offend if you believe them to be true to begin with.

In his book *The Fire from Within*, author, Carlos Castaneda, claims he was told these words, "Self importance is man's greatest enemy. What weakens him is feeling offended by the deeds and misdeeds of his fellow man. Self-importance requires that one spend most of one's life offended by something or someone."

In my early twenties, I worked with a lady who was always on the lookout for offenders. In her opinion, the co-workers were all out to get her. When hearing her side of a story, I quickly learned that she was way off base about the intentions of others. Her ears always heard the message in a mean or nasty tone. She didn't sleep well because at night she had to plot to reclaim her importance the next day. Her world was a dangerous one, filled with lions and tigers and bears. Oh my.

Work on changing your perception of the motives of others. If you think someone is trying to intentionally hurt you, then give him or her the benefit of the doubt. Don't be a complete fool, however. Occasionally, you'll run across the paths of those that have the capacity to cause you considerable harm. If you find one, just turn the other way.

Focus on your purpose, and the talents given you to fulfill that purpose. Don't give your tormentor any more ammunition. Remember Dolly Parton and your silver slippers. And, oh yes, send forth love!

Become the Adult

I've really had to come to terms with the fact I am now a walking and talking *adult*.

—C.S. Lewis

A psychological study done around the seventies asked a large number of mental health practitioners to separately define mentally healthy adults, men and women. The definition for men and adults were the same. The definition of a mentally healthy woman was completely different. The mindset was women who acted like adults weren't playing nice.

By definition, the Queen is an adult. Usually when you are experiencing energy draining emotions that keep you blocked, you have in some way given away parts of yourself. You have acquiesced your Self as a frightened child. Good. Here is a tremendous opportunity to remember where your personal power truly resides…you know, the power God gave you to fulfill your purpose.

Make a list of those qualities you think a mentally healthy adult possesses. For example, I think a mentally healthy adult does not have to ask permission to do what she wants to do. She may have to make arrangements, but that is merely part of being responsible, another mentally healthy adult quality. A mentally healthy adult does not have to lie about her purchases. A mentally responsible adult does not have to get angry or sad before she is allowed to do what she wants to.

Even though you are clearing the way to fulfill your idea of a mentally responsible adult, take baby steps. See first where you are *not* being the adult in your life. Then try it. If you were Queen, what would you do? Hint: The answer is *not* off with their heads.

Another barrier to accessing your Queenly personal authority is fear-based emotions. Noted author Maggie Scarf who has done a body of work on relationships developed the 'genogram.' It's an emotional family tree, and she hypothesizes that trauma in past generations repeats itself in current relationships. This works on many levels. If one of your parents had an issue with money, you are more likely to repeat it with your spouse. If one of your parents was emotionally abandoned or isolated, you may find you or your children experiencing the same issue. This is why looking at family history and exploring family narrative is so important. It's so much harder to change your story about the way the world works, if you don't know the story you inherited.

If talking about money arouses fear-based emotions in you, look back. Was this a problem in your family? Try to pinpoint ways your parents felt about money, and try to determine if the basis for their concerns is pertinent in your situation, or if you are creating your current reality from old stories that aren't really about you.

Sometimes, just looking at family dynamics is enough to help you remember you are still wearing your silver slippers. You have been endowed with personal authority, power and choice for a purpose—your divine purpose.

While you are clearing out old fear-based emotional patterns, and teaching yourself to claim adult status, please remember, nobody else has to change for this to happen. Victoria Axline in her modern classic *Dibs In Search of Self* detailed her work with a young boy who isolated himself from everyone and attacked anyone who came near him. His mother allowed Axline to work with him, on the condition that neither of the parents would participate. It was obvious to Axline, Dibs was trapped in his own world, terrified of the outside world, because of his parents' way of coping with their lives and emotions. During play therapy, Axline helped Dibs look at his relationships with his parents, and experience his own fear-based emotions. As the rules with which his parents governed his world emerged, he began to heal.

Axline did not give him emotional comfort, because she knew he would have to return to his world without her. He had to learn to come to terms with his own emotions himself. He did. And as he changed, his parents changed. They became more loving and responsive. Dibs, almost violently autistic when Axline met him, grew into a gifted and loving young man.

If a child can change his world, so can we. It's time we reclaimed our protective energy. We have been given a purpose. It's time we remembered our silver slippers, and choose to use them to fulfill that purpose. It's time we emerge as Queen.

Love

Love is everything it's cracked up to be. That's why people are so cynical about it. It really is worth fighting for, being brave for, risking everything for. And the trouble is, if you don't risk anything, you risk even more.

—Erica Jong

Now that we are working through forgiveness, are learning to be gentle with ourselves, and are assuming the grown-up role, here's a major hint. Most people want you to love or appreciate them. Others know when we don't love them unconditionally. And, as evidenced in earlier discussions, most of us don't have the capacity to love others without conditions yet. I know I've struggled with learning how to do this. No matter how hard I try, I still find myself judging someone based on inconsequential things like appearance, accent, shyness. I learned over time that my evaluation doesn't have to be an indication of love. Instead, I try to look at my literal mind's interpretation 'the judger' as only a review—and not a deciding factor of whether I like, dislike or love someone. With practice, it gets easier, but even now I find myself needing to turn off the inner critic.

I'm not sure why we learned to process others this way, but we did. My eight-year-old daughter recently cried about being different from her friends. She responded to my consoling: "But Mom, I don't want to be different from the others." Why not? Does she already recognize that being different means you are less likely to be loved? I was the age my daughter is now when I got my first taste of knowing that not everyone loved everyone else. One of our neighborhood friends liked me better than she did my sister. Poor Suzanne. She was always getting hit in the head with toys. This aggressive little friend never hit me. Why was that? Did I look different? Act differently? Did our little friend not feel appreciated by my sister?

Extend love to everyone in your life. Work hard to continue to demonstrate loving feelings for all living creatures. You want love, too. You'll get more of it by putting it out there. Have you ever left another's company second-guessing yourself? Feeling unworthy? Doubting yourself?

Sure you have. I have. I hypothesize that when this happens you have found yourself in the presence of a judger. Your intuition perked up and supplied you with a warning.

The only problem is that you don't have the skill to figure out those negative feelings didn't come from you—that, instead they came from another—an external influence.

The best way to combat the judger is by sending out love. It's as simple as: I love you. Those times when you have a hard time mustering up the good old love feelings or your mind chatters about how another person offends you, just keep saying to yourself: "I love you. I love you."

Perhaps Erica Jong was speaking of romantic love when she said love is worth the risk. But in reality love is a natural condition of living, of being. To continually send thoughts of love to someone you perceive doesn't love you really is worth the risk. You are siding with the basic Truth at the heart of Life. And the love you extend will always return to you. As Erica says, if you don't risk it, you risk even more.

Continue to monitor your 'bad' feelings. Loving another person whom you perceive is treating you badly, doesn't mean you must accept abuse. If you constantly experience self-doubt in the company of a specific individual—if you can—avoid that person. Years ago, I worked for a man who judged everyone and everybody all the time. It was constant. I know because he had a negative comment to make about everyone that entered his office. Of course, I knew that those judgments applied to me as well. I wasn't naïve enough to believe that I was off limits. Physically drained after each interaction, I was thrilled when he was away from the office. To this day, I am not sure if I was simply picking up on his depression (the big black cloud that followed him around) or if it was bad vibes he was sending out to me, and anyone else who invaded his space. Finally, I realized I had to get away and I did. Whew! He wasn't related to me, so I could choose to avoid him at all costs.

As you structure a healthier reality, you will surround yourself with people that make you feel good—people that love and care about you.

Learning to forgive, learning to drop judgments of yourself and others, learning to assume the role of adult in your own life, and learning to give and receive love clears the way for your authentic self to emerge. Once all the negative energy that has been blocking you is released, you will find you are moving forward with zest. You have accessed the power that indeed makes you a Queen.

CHAPTER THIRTEEN

Claiming the Throne

For so long power has been a matter of control and dominion, the thing that keeps some people up and others down, the blood that feeds the hierarchy. The kind of power women need is not ruthless, controlling, self-serving, dominion-seeking power—power without benefit of love. It is not staying up to keep others down. What we need is a potent, forceful power, yes, but one that is also compassionate, that enables others as well.

—Sue Monk Kidd

Mirror, Mirror on the Wall

IN *SNOW WHITE*, The Wicked Stepmother looked in the mirror every day, or maybe more. Maybe every time she thought the king was ignoring her, or the servants were surly, or when she was laughing, she accidentally snorted. "Who's the fairest of them all?"

"You are, My Queen," the mirror would answer, until one day, maybe the day she had eaten an extra serving of tiramisu—oops, we are in the

Mississippi Delta—make that hot fudge cake, with ice cream—and she went to the mirror, and asked the question, and this time the mirror answered, "Snow White is a thousand times lovelier than you."

I bet you could hear the shriek all the way to Jackson. Snow White… that Good Little Girl, well on her way to growing up and seizing the throne. It's no wonder the Wicked Stepmother told the henchman to bring back Snow White's heart.

Because it was Snow White's heart that told the Wicked Stepmother she was good, no matter if she chortled and spit when she laughed, even if she ate *all* of the hot fudge cake, even if nobody cared if she were good or bad, or even worse, nobody noticed.

Who put the curse on little Briar Rose? That dratted Sleeping Beauty? The fairy who was *not* invited to the celebration because the castle was one gold plate shy. When did the spell take place? Just as the young girl was on her way to becoming a woman, full of her own power.

And the Wicked Witch of the West and Dorothy! Dorothy had the magic shoes of great power, and wouldn't give them up.

Here is the secret. In each of us is a young woman on the verge of her power. In each of us is a Wicked Stepmother Witch, who offers the curse.

Now, the real secret. What do all these fairy stories have in common? Snow White *must* accept the poisoned laces and comb. She *must* eat the poisoned apple. Sleeping Beauty *must* reach out and touch the spindle. And the Witch cannot just kill Dorothy and take her shoes. Dorothy is safe unless she takes the shoes off on her own.

A Queen You're Not

I got a witch mad at me, and you might get into trouble.

—Dorothy, *Wizard of Oz*

When the Scarecrow asked Dorothy if he could travel with her to Oz to ask the Wizard for brains, she understood her predicament perfectly. If a witch is mad, everyone should expect trouble.

For a brief time in my life, I worked for a woman who *thought* she was a queen. She took every opportunity, in a private meeting or with all employees present, to declare how powerful she was. Her power and her abilities to sway others impressed her. I can imagine her going home at night and looking in the mirror, asking the old question, expecting the coveted answer.

"Allyn, I have to be careful what I say," she said in an uneventful meeting one day. "You know how much *personal* power I have."

Clue number one. If you have to tell people how powerful you are, you probably are not.

It never failed, and no matter the setting, the boss made reference to her power. At the same time she made every effort to diminish the power of others. Designating herself 'all powerful,' she ruled with a sword. She fired people at will. She created elaborate schemes to keep her little bees busy. The environment she created was sick and dysfunctional.

She was the Queen who felt her safety lay in force.

Arrogant, unkind, unforgiving, vengeful, vane, selfish, hard, moody. Ice Queen, Drama Queen, Queen of Mean, Queen of Sin, Queen of Pain. This dark aspect of the Queen archetype is portrayed in many fairy tales. She must use black magic to weave her spells, and rule by force and manipulation. She demands complete adoration. Today, people who exhibit these characteristics are destructive forces, and usually cause misery for their family and co-workers.

Owning Your Authentic, But Queenly Power

The problem with the Queen archetype is that it frightens us. Women typically don't know how to comfortably embrace their power. Historically, we have witnessed abuse of power by both men and women. Our model for claiming power is distorted and misrepresents the way that is 'right' to handle ourselves.

We often feel we have two choices. To be the Princess, eager to please and perform, to be perfectly what the world tells us we should be. Or to be the Wicked Stepmother, with angry red nails as sharp as claws, and a cruel smile, full of deceit and wrath.

Both the Perfect Princess and the Wicked Stepmother, or Wicked Queen, emerge from the same source. They have forgotten who they are. The Princess must hide everything that doesn't meet the approval of Authority. The Wicked Queen deluded by power will use force. And be mad that she must. The Wicked Queen is the Princess who can no longer live with the pain of hiding the Unlived Life.

It is when we invite our Shadow Self out into the light, when we understand we were born with power, and in order to fulfill our purpose, we must claim it, that we start a story that begins, "Once upon a time there lived a powerful Queen…"

So if the Princess is a Pleaser, and the Wicked Queen is a Punisher, what are the qualities of Powerful Queen?

Power is personal. If you read my definition, and create a list of *shoulds* and *should nots*, you will have given away your authentic power. But I do offer you my list, the one that's worked for me. It will be a starting point for you.

As you read and consider, you will begin to see your own life, and notice where you are denying your Unlived Life, and how you can invite her into the light. You will discover you can quickly recognize when her voice is calling to you. It will be when you feel sad, or angry, or afraid. And you will also notice when you have heard her, and heeded, for you will feel peace and joy, and it won't depend on anything outside yourself—not chocolate, not drugs, not other people and how they behave. You will be energized and eager for today and tomorrow. You will have awakened. You will be whole. You have claimed your right to be Queen.

The Authentic Queen

The Authentic Queen is Powerful. A Queen recognizes and understands her power. She claims it and doesn't apologize for having it. She is inner directed and follows her heart.

151

Cultural influences, specifically a Southern culture, set me up to be afraid of other people who possessed more power than I did. And as a good Princess—that included everyone.

Up until my early thirties, the people I deemed most powerful were professional men. Men in suits scared me most. For some reason, the minute I saw one I handed it all over. "Here, please take it. It's yours." To get over my fear, I continually placed myself in positions to challenge my fear. Not entirely by design, I found myself speaking to professional men or working in jobs surrounded by men in suits. In one job, I regularly talked to judges—a solid archetypal representation of power.

My biggest lesson was learning not to immediately surrender my power in a situation. The next lesson was realizing that power didn't automatically place one in an adversarial role. The men in suits weren't the enemy. The men in suits could be on your team.

I also had to deal with cultural perceptions of women in power. It's ugly. The powerful woman is cold, hard and wicked. She doesn't care who or what is standing in her way, she'll get to where she's going. If you simply happen to be in the way, look out. It's all about winning at all costs with no regard to hurting others along the way. This image scared me, too. I didn't want to be the cutthroat bitch portrayed on television.

To get to a place to believe having and showing power was okay, I had to find others doing it the *right* way. That was a tough challenge, but I found them. I used those early mentors to shape my ideas. I then modeled their behavior, by saying things to myself like, "What would Lois do in this situation?" Or, "How would Dr. Kirkland handle this?"

I also learned from the mistakes of others. Remember the female boss that needed to tell everyone how powerful she was? Only with the group for nine months, I learned volumes about what *not* to do.

One of the misnomers concerning power is when people link it with control. At that point it becomes force. Power increases energy by combining the energy of all individuals working together. Force destroys energy. It requires all the energy to be expended on keeping other people in line.

Possessing personal power does not mean you control others—their behaviors, their actions or their responses. People that have to tell you they are powerful either by declaration or by force are not. When the need to control takes over, you are dancing as hard as you can so no one will discover you are a fake Queen with no power.

Personal or authentic power is not about controlling others or outcomes. It's about confidence, intuition and listening to an inner voice. People with personal power glow. You recognize them. You know who they are. And when you are proceeding from your authentic self, your whole self, you have become the Queen.

The Authentic Queen is Inner-directed. A Queen takes direction from her heart, not her intellect. Ignoring the good opinion of others a Queen acts using her intuition.

I first heard the term 'good opinion of others' while listening to Wayne Dyer, bestselling author and lecturer. I had been affected by the 'good opinion of others' all my life, so his comments resonated with me. It's the approval issue. We aren't born into this world needing it, but we come out of childhood craving it. We care about what others think to the detriment of ourselves. We drown out our internal voices because we worry that who we are will not match up—will make us unlovable.

If you recall, my eight-year-old daughter is already discovering the opinion of others. It's heartbreaking to watch. While her concern about what she says and thinks, or how she looks is part of a process, it also brings up bad memories for my husband and me. "Yep, first grade is when I started to care about what others thought," my husband recently reminisced.

I think my appreciation of external judgment started in second grade when it was clear that all the other children didn't have as much arm hair as I did. I fretted about it. Cried about it. Even asked my mother to take me to the doctor. The doctor wasn't much help, though. He said something like, "You need to dye and cut it regularly." We tried the trimming thing for a while, but my arms always looked worse—gaps of hair missing were much more obvious than leaving it be. My daughter is facing the same challenge. She too, has more arm hair than her classmates.

One day recently she cried to me, "I want to be just like everyone else. Why do I have to be different?" I asked her if others had pointed out her imperfections and she responded, "No."

My case had been different. I was laughed at. Called a gorilla and an ape. That's what pushed me to seek medical assistance. Addy's pain is self-inflicted at the moment. Later, it might be the opinion of others that push her to take more drastic measures. In the meantime, I am saddened by the fact that our children believe it's wrong to be different when in reality there are more differences than likenesses.

All during elementary school it seems the focus is on what's wrong with a person. As a defense, children copy the group they like the most. It's a new family intent on having *all* in common, of finding comfort and security by being *alike*. Differences, then, are diminished by force—straightening curly hair, dyeing dark arm hair, dieting, acting out against innate feelings and emotions. The child that gets picked on, turns out, is the child that is *most* different.

We carry these old wounds into adulthood and continue to pick on the weak or different. Even those we thought were most popular were wounded by the game. No matter the reason, we are encouraged to fit our square pegs into round holes. We are encouraged to mute our own desires, needs and magnificent differences to fit into the whole. The process is warped. The damage is irrefutable.

Walking by Addy's side, I have an opportunity to look at these old hurts, at the way I twisted myself to be like everyone else. I am still learning to turn inward, to trust my *differences* were given to me as a divine gift at my birth.

Perhaps our need to be *alike* is a herd instinct, urging us to group together for safety. And it works. As a species we have survived. But the major changes that have occurred in civilization, the startling advances, the holiest wisdoms bestowed on us, were revealed by people who were *different*. We are all divinely *different*. And when we begin to live from our innermost truth, we have accepted those gifts, and have become Queen.

The Authentic Queen Recognizes She Is Special. A Queen intuitively knows that there is nothing wrong with understanding her God-given grace and talents. She confidently maneuvers life while focusing on her uniqueness.

Nothing is wrong with feeling special. Quite frankly, minus the feeling, you might not develop self-worth. Everyone is unique and therefore, is special. We all have something 'important' to do—live our lives. According to David Hawkins: "There is a normal, benign level of pride that is more correctly termed 'self-esteem' or 'self-care.' This refers to putting one's best foot forward and the normal satisfaction that results from successful effort and achievement." He adds, "They (forms of positive self image) have been earned and have a realistic foundation."

Be somebody. I tell my little friends that, "Be somebody!" Oh how proud you can make yourself. Pride in oneself is such a marvelous attribute.

—Viola, 83 years old

As a young child, I understood the importance of being special—deep within myself, I felt loved and appreciated for the person I was. All too soon, however, the demands of my culture took that all away from me. In one article I described the experience. Here is an excerpt:

I remember playing dress up when I was a small child. One early spring, right after turning five, the idea of being a Queen consumed me. I wore my tiara everywhere. Not only that, but I was also happy. It felt good to be a Queen. It felt good to recognize who I was. I was special. Yes. I was special. My parents showered me with compliments and praise, and taught me from an early age how good it felt to be adored. I had doting uncles and aunts that cared about and for me. I was special in the eyes of many.

In response to my queenly feelings, my mother filled an oversized box with clothes and costume jewelry fit for a monarch. Daily I adorned myself in vibrant hues—fuchsia, red, yellow—and wore flashy costume jewels—emeralds, rubies, diamonds. To complement my accessories, I dressed in only the most extravagant garb and fabric wraps—scraps of velvet, cotton and paisley prints mother used to sew our patterned dresses. Knowing that all queens must have a red velvet robe, scepter

and tiara, my mother used her imagination to give me all I needed to be truly regal.

As I approached adolescence my tiara began to slip, and I lost sight of that perfect me. It all was blurred between trying to please others, following the rules and being myself. The distance between my parents and me grew as is typical during adolescence. No longer a friendly shoulder, they were now distant and uninviting. In my eyes they had changed. In hindsight, I was the one that closed the door—buried my emotions and fled. Changes in my physical appearance, infused with a surge of hormones, sent me spiraling on a downward path…

It was during the downward spiral that I lost sight of how special I was. Yes, I was indeed a special person—in the eyes of the God who created me, I was worthy of being loved. Carefully evaluate your opinion, however, to avoid replacing your self-worth with self-importance. With the notion of self-importance comes the idea that somehow or another we are better than others. We are not. Let's return to what Carlos Castaneda said about self-importance: "Self-importance requires that one spends most of one's life offended by something or someone."

During the years I was trying to find myself, I made the mistake of thinking I was special in a superior way. I had better manners. Handled my affairs competently. Won most people over. Blah, blah, blah. My distorted ideas led me to seek all the wrong things—such as trudging through traditional jobs and currying the good opinions of others. I couldn't have said it better than Wayne Dyer in *The Power of Intention,* "True nobility isn't about being better than someone else. It's about being better than you used to be."

Seeking nobility, a Queen recognizes she is special—not in comparison to others, but in her own right. A Queen does not seek to dominate others. Claiming her right to lead herself, she naturally leads. A Queen seeks to grow and improve Honoring the specialness of her own, she rejoices in the specialness of others.

An Authentic Queen remains Steady. She diligently strives to strike balance in all facets of her life—spiritual, family, career, play.

In *Raising Up Queens*, Ester Davis-Thompson refers to our many responsibilities and duties as woman-work. She says, "Part of our charge is to create our home spaces—and, if we choose to have children, it's the nest we make." She further explains, "The balance we need for our lives will come when we take the time to look within for our answers…A comfortable rhythm of work…give…ponder…rest…will arise if we are willing to be flexible."

From observation, I recognize many women struggle to devote time and energy to all in their charge while also keeping up work-related activities, social commitments and spiritual pursuits. Numerous Queen Power forum posts tell us that too often a woman puts herself last.

Like the Red Queen already mentioned by my friend, Viola, "You have to run everyday so very, very hard just to stay in place." Modernizing the phrase a little it seems more appropriate to say, "just to catch up." During one lighthearted discussion on the forums, I mentioned having a Red Queen week. "Yes, I'm going to be a Purple Queen next week—a queen that meets her deadlines, keeps herself on task while stopping now and then to do stuff that she enjoys."

Kelly, one of our forum Queens responded, "I hear you! I've been a Red Queen myself, lately. What color are you when you just have too much on your plate, but you have to eat all of it anyway, without letting anything drip or fall off?"

Balancing our lives, caring for our loved-ones, keeping on task, meeting deadlines, tending the house—takes so much.

My friend Terrie shared in one of our blogs, "I have three children under the age of ten. Of course since July, I've been waiting for school to start. Well, thank goodness for Labor Day Holiday so we can sleep in! Church? Ha! That's when we can all catch up on our sleep! And, when is that next summer break? Now my days are filled with stressing about carpools, getting to school on time, cafeteria duty, library duty, supply room duty, potty duty! Does it ever end? Did I fail to mention that I squeeze working in there somewhere? Yes, in a wonderful, relaxing aromatherapy bath—any salts will do. Calgon, take me away…This Red Queen is tired." And, my friend Terrie will be the first to tell you that it's usually self-care and her personal projects that take a backseat.

She's right, it is *typically* self-care that falls by the way even though women understand its importance and significance. In another post Kelly said, "Yesterday, for example, I learned once again that when I treat myself like a Queen, I feel like one…Quite possibly, the inspiration for yesterday's re-realization? A massage, plus the hair salon worked on my Queenly coif. Sounds kind of superficial, I know, but it's not. How I feel about myself after receiving a royal treatment goes WAY deeper than my new 'do'."

Another Queen told us, "I can see (even though I'm only 40 and my kids are 9 and 7) that I will have to work at NOT becoming an angry, resentful mom! It's easy to fall into the routine of doing what is right and important for everyone else in the family. (I mean, how else do you keep the harmony and tranquility in the midst?) However, it is amazing how different things are when I do take time for myself (and therefore am happier at home). I tell my kids quite often, 'When I am happy, you will be happy.' It really is important to love yourself first—if not you, then who will?" Equate that to a similar phrase and follow-up question: It's really important to take care of yourself first—if not, then who will? No one usually takes care of the caregiver.

In addition to self-care, we have to turn our attention to our dreams and aspirations, our own spiritual growth. This can never be repeated too often, and this time the inclusion of a *must* seems most appropriate: Carving out moments to allow reflective thought, hair appointments, reading time, hot soaking baths is essential to your well-being and health. Really, "When *you* are happy, then *they* will be happy."

Yes…it's hard to grow when the children need attention, baths, help with their studies, dinner, lunch money, a red shirt for the school program, Christmas, a new computer, a clarinet, a dance class, a pair of cleats…and some discipline. For this week. But…growth is how you will get to your High Places. So when your Inner Woman, who is in charge of growth, asks for just a little of your attention…just a bit of your time…for you to slow down and get still sometime soon…consider, won't you, penciling her into your schedule?

—Ester Davis-Thompson

So, now it's time to just breathe. I love the analogy of the oxygen mask.

If a woman has to choose between catching a fly ball and saving an infant's life, she will choose to save the infant's life without even considering if there are men on base.

—Dave Barry

When you fly, the stewardess instructs us to place the oxygen mask on our faces before helping our children with theirs. The directives go against our maternal instincts. Right? Isn't our first impulse to save the children? The message tells us by saving our own lives first we have more power and ability to save the lives of our children.

The first step *is* to save ourselves. We do this by paying attention to our needs—what makes me happy? What do I need to be a better person? I know that I am now a better mother to my daughter. Why? Because I am happier, a more fulfilled person.

Being so significantly reduces my anger, frustration and sadness. The journey can be short or long, direct or indirect. No matter the length or the level of difficulty, the journey will happen. So, why not take the journey with our eyes wide open? Why not jump in with the intention of saving ourselves, because in doing so, we are saving the lives of our children?

An Authentic Queen is Focused on Partnering. A Queen wants to collaborate and to join forces. She brings relationships with others front and center while encouraging independence in herself and others.

For the longest time, I attempted to do most everything by myself. I'm not sure why or when I decided that was the best way to get my needs met, but I did. Somewhere along the path, I declared, "Enough! I will just do it myself." To me, the world was incompetent—words of a former perfectionist speaking here.

Perfectionists are usually loners. Without help from others, the journey is extended and quite frankly, more dangerous. The shortest distance from one point to the next is not a straight line—it's people.

Many people take a different path and decide they are the incompetent ones. Taking this stance, they rely on others to get anything done *right*. The latter group sometimes appears to have lots of friends, but often feels they are in danger, also. Too unsure of themselves to take a stand, they must cling to the herd. And sometimes being scared and unsure makes them very sad.

Many of us have a mixture of both…and seesaw back and forth.

A Queen lives on the middle ground. She seeks enough assistance to move forward while using her independence to stay on track and follow inner guidance.

Family and friends are very important to the Queen. She spends time nurturing all-important relationships while supporting individual autonomy. Recognizing success benefits everyone. She applauds the success of others as well enjoying her own.

The Authentic Queen is Empathetic and Kind. A Queen cares about others. She is compassionate to the point of taking action to assist family, friends and strangers.

An Authentic Queen can imagine walking in the shoes of others. She is interested in her community, whether that encompasses only her immediate family or the greater community of town, state and country. Quick to defend, the Queen stands behind just and moral living without carrying the burden of judgment in her back pocket.

When I was five years old and much queenlier, I absolutely understood that I needed to be considerate and kind to others. I acted on this belief without question or without regard to what others thought.

One day, my kindergarten classmates and I were gathered on the front porch of the house that accommodated our classroom. My quiet, shy friend flipped over the edge and fell face down in the bushes. All my classmates laughed at her. They wouldn't stop. I was outraged. Folly Ann, due to her introverted nature, wouldn't speak up, but I sure did. The whole time I spoke, I wasn't worried one bit about what they thought or if they'd like me anymore. It didn't matter. What happened to Folly Ann wasn't right. That is what mattered.

Later in my life, I forgot to be empathetic. I dropped compassion, for the most part, to impress my friends. If all my friends were comforting someone, then heck, I could too. But, never during my middle school years, did I take a lone stand for truth and integrity.

A Queen is more concerned about helping others than worrying about what inconsequential friends or strangers will think. Despite what the fairy tales say, a Queen never seeks revenge. Revenge is the defense of the powerless.

She addresses issues straight on and handles all conflict in an open manner. A Queen knows that meaningful relationships are developed and maintained by remaining true to oneself, and empathy and kindness are gifts to share with those you love.

An Authentic Queen Is Decisive. A Queen makes strong-minded decisions. She might take her time or quickly investigate prospective solutions, but ultimately she makes up her mind. A Queen knows that making a mistake is a learning process and does not fear making the wrong choice.

Gathering too much information can be detrimental to the decision-making process. On the flipside, not taking time to evaluate pertinent information can, too. Again, a Queen finds the middle ground and works from that vantage point. As a young adult, I hated it when I was caught making a mistake, particularly at work. I would do anything, even lie, to cover up my weakness. Although never one to shy away from making a decision, I sometimes moved too quickly and caused myself undue pain. Topping my overly resolute behavior with the need to be perfect meant that I experienced severe anguish.

Wallowing in indecision is not a queenly thing to do either. Whether the cause is a need to gather too much information or a weak backbone, waiting too long equals missed opportunities and frustrated collaborators. Both are symptoms of believing all power resides with others, not within. A Queen reviews the situation while considering the facts. She then moves forward.

It's sort of like the game of tennis. In community league play, the player calls his or her own lines. Sometimes you make bad calls and sometimes you make good ones. If you make a call that your opponent doesn't agree with, you don't say, "Oh, did I make a mistake?" even if you start second-guessing yourself, "Maybe I did mess that one up." You just stick to your decision. In tennis, the feedback regarding your decisions is immediate. You know within seconds if the opponent is happy or if they *think* you messed up.

And, similar to tennis, a Queen understands that you win some and you lose some, but it usually all works out in the end. Go with the facts as you know them. Make timely decisions and act swiftly to correct bad decisions as needed. Relax, follow your intuition, and with scepter in hand, make up your mind.

An Authentic Queen Is Succinct and Direct. A Queen makes clear, short and snappy points. She understands other people's time is valuable.

Being succinct means being concise and timely when giving information or making requests. Being verbose and unclear are merely ways of covering up a lack of personal power. You may instead be using words to manipulate the other person into agreeing with you, rather than stating your needs or ideas clearly, and taking the chance others might question you.

There is a time and place for narrative, for going the long way to get home. It's one way we understand the world. But when we act, we don't need to apologize for being decisive. A Queen speaks out, and knows she is worthy of being heard.

The Authentic Queen Is Accepting. A Queen accepts others without judgment or preconceived notions. She thinks before speaking and makes every effort to avoid game playing. A Queen speaks from her heart while still holding on to her empathetic nature. She loves people for their differences while recognizing most people are not out to hurt or damage.

A Queen gives everyone the benefit of the doubt. Even if a Queen thinks she's been slighted or unjustly treated, she graciously offers another chance to the offending party. She provides numerous opportunities to those appearing to cause harm. Instead of seeking revenge, a Queen removes herself from harm's way, moving to higher and safer ground until the danger passes. If the offensive person is someone she cannot escape, she confronts him or her head on while using a kind hand. When a Queen discusses a problem with another person, she uses truth *and* love. A Queen takes the high road when dealing with others.

It's not about using power, smarts or finesse to manipulate others. It's about using clear and straightforward language to communicate your opinion and concerns. When listening to others share their ideas, the queenly thing to do is give them the benefit of the doubt. The motivating factor for most folks is getting their needs met—not to hurt or manipulate you. Most miscommunication stems from our inability to comprehend the motivation. Assume that all individuals you meet have only good intentions and you'll find that *most* do.

Again, referring to the game of tennis, I like to give opponents the chance to make the error or the great shot. If they smoke a shot down the alley (on the edge of the court and past me), I think, "Good shot." If they do it again, then I pay more attention to the alley I'm guarding. If they do it a third time, I know they can hurt me at will.

The same goes for communication and putting yourself out there. If someone seems to send you a zinger, don't assume that it was.

If she does it again, take notice. If she does it a third time, then she is a half-conscious Queen, thinking her power lies in overpowering you. She is playing defensively by being aggressively offensive. She is one of those folks that doesn't have your best intentions at heart and will continue to hurt you.

Anyone taking the low road is still trying to get her needs met, but simply is going about it the wrong way. No matter the cause, the queenly path involves sticking to a direct plan in all communications—meaning, no maltreatment or game playing. Avoid those that don't play fair if you can. If you can't, kindly uncover the deception by openly questioning them. If necessary, ask for an explanation in front of others. Avoid the temptation to humiliate or embarrass. Instead, keep the focus on clarifying the situation.

You are Queen. Like Dorothy and her silver slippers, you have the protective energy of inner authority. Unless you give it away, you cannot be harmed.

An Authentic Queen Is Warm-hearted and Generous. A Queen has a giving, generous and warm heart. She is not focused on scarcity. She isn't afraid to give and to love.

Queens must have cold hands, because the saying goes—"Cold hands, warm heart." There is no ice running through the veins of a Queen. She loves others with her whole heart and demonstrates to them her warmhearted love by her demeanor, greetings and sincerity. She has no hidden agenda and only wants others to feel loved and comfortable in her presence. A Queen will bend over backwards to help another relax in her warmth.

I learned about the art of giving from my Dad and father-in-law. My Dad gives by picking up the tab or paying more than his share. He never questions the motives of others, but simply pays what needs to be paid. He doesn't hold a grudge or ask that others pay more next time. He, plainly put, is generous—he expects nothing in return.

My father-in-law was also a very generous man. He gave money away all the time. He would give it to us—sharing evenly with all his children the proceeds from selling a car or chopping down timber. Mr. Evans also gave his time. He spent hours visiting sick folks. The nurses at the local hospital knew him on a first name basis. Not because he was a patient, but because he was always there spending time with the sick. He didn't care if he knew the patient or not. Probably his greatest gift was getting others to laugh or smile. If he didn't have a small gift to give you, he always had a joke to tell.

When we give, we must give out of our own abundance, not because we expect someone to reciprocate or love us more. Giving is not about "what all I've done for you lately," or because you expect something in return. Knowing how to give without expecting anything in return is the queenly way to live. My father and father-in-law showed me how to do this by example.

True giving is not currency to purchase the good opinion of others. It does not endanger the giver, nor the people she or he is responsible for. My father gave out of abundance. Abundance is also the source of my father-in-law's generosity. When we give, we too must give out of our own abundance. If our finances are tight, then we can give of our love…a smile, a hug, a kind word. Queenly giving never requires the giver to sacrifice.

Queens are more than generous for they understand that what is given away usually returns threefold to the giver.

An Authentic Queen Keeps Her Promises. A Queen makes every effort to keep her word. A Queen knows that if she can't, then she explains herself, and states the reason for not following through.

Most of us were taught to keep our word. Queens take the lesson seriously. If you give your word carelessly, when you break it others will doubt you. That's not the real problem.

The real problem is that you learn to doubt yourself. You do not think your power lies within, with your intentions. You believe it belongs to other people and circumstances out of your control. If you can't trust yourself, you become dependent on others to dictate to you.

If by chance a Queen is unable to keep her word, she remembers to be clear and concise stating the reason why. She does not have to hide her actions, or manipulate others to retain their good opinion. Sometimes life happens, as they say, and we must change our plans.

A Queen knows her given word carries with it all the power she is endowed with. Even before spoken aloud, a Queen gives her word to herself first.

An Authentic Queen Is Truthful. A Queen tries her very best to tell the truth understanding it is much more tiresome to lie or gossip. A Queen grasps that on some level others can sense untruths or deception and seeks to be honest in all relationships.

Our culture teaches us to lie or to misrepresent the truth. For years, I used lying to make myself look better and to avoid hurting feelings. Lying to cover mistakes was easy. Very similar to the *Family Circle* cartoon, "Not me! I didn't do it," I used lying to protect myself, to get by and to impress others. Telling others what they wanted to hear or believe about me was easier than telling the truth. Not wanting to hurt others, I lied to explain why I said no to them or to hide my *real* opinions. Never before strong enough to simply say, "I'm not interested in doing that;" or, "I'd rather stay at home and not do anything;" or, "I'd rather be alone;" I created elaborate stories that, more times than not, ended up hurting me. Remembering who knows what and who doesn't is awfully draining. And, ensuring that your partner can back you up on the mental reservation, the lie that goes around the truth can be dreadfully traumatic.

I know, darn it, I'm taking all the fun out of *not* playing with others. As much fun as getting away with pulling the wool over someone's eyes is, though, it makes you feel bad, and it drains your energy. Every time you say something negative or untrue about another, not only do you zap your energy, but you take a little of theirs, too.

For the most part, I don't lie anymore. Whew! That was a tough habit to kick. I also rarely gossip, but again, find myself sometimes saying something that either I can't substantiate, or I know is unkind.

I try to remember gossiping is like trying to get a pair of silver slippers by stealing them from someone else. Gossip is always judgmental...a "we are more powerful because we are right, and *they* are oh! so wrong" kind of thing.

Most of the time I can make myself stop. I redirect my comments or take them back. But, there are still times that I can't help it. I know exactly what I'm doing. My little voice warns me of the infraction, but I keep going—feeling terrible afterwards and asking silently the other person's forgiveness. I am confident that soon I will be taking the high road and my lying and gossiping habits will be long forgotten. I can't wait!

Toss out the fact that deceit is definitely not a good thing to do—there are plenty of other reasons to swear off lying altogether. All the stories sooner or later will catch up with you—making you look deceitful and dishonest in front of others. Eventually, people will figure it out and the damage is usually irreconcilable. Going on past behavior, you have demonstrated that you tell lies. The past is a good indicator of the future—

meaning if you lied once, you would probably lie again. Not only that, but others on some intuitive level pick up on your deceit. Although not exactly sure why, they simply don't trust you. They sense you are not telling the truth and therefore, do not have their best interests at heart. You, by lying, have a hidden agenda. You are trying to manipulate them.

But the most dangerous effect of lying is you are creating a false identity to present to the world. Nobody knows the real you, so you feel sad, isolated and frightened, even if you lie so nobody will find out.

A Queen is authentic. She owns her life. She knows by telling the truth, whether anybody else does or not, she knows who she is.

An Authentic Queen Is Forgiving and Merciful. A Queen forgives everyone for everything. She understands that holding a grudge is not beneficial and seeking revenge causes harm to all involved.

All right, we are repeating this lesson. But it is a very important one to learn. It's hard to forgive and forget, especially when you are on the receiving end. After deciding to forgive everyone that I had ever held responsible for my wounds, it took me days to go through the list. The longer you've lived, the longer the list. Some of the transgressors hurt you purposely and others did not. No matter the category, forgiveness is a must.

The most important person to forgive, however, is yourself. When evaluating the wrongs committed by others, you also must review your contribution to the pain. It normally takes at least two attempts, and many times there are no innocent victims. We all play parts whether it is being the victim, the saboteur or the vengeful monster.

The flipside of this forgiveness business is that you need to consider all the individuals that you have unintentionally caused pain.

It goes back to forgiving yourself. Whether you ask the person directly or say a prayer of forgiveness privately, a Queen always seeks reckoning for missteps.

Now here is the secret elixir to forgiveness. If you think you are harmed, you have voluntarily given away your silver slippers. You have given up your power to another person, to a harmful situation. But this is an illusion. *You can't give away your silver slippers.* But you can pretend you have. And then you hobble though life, the captive of the Wicked Witch of the West.

Now try it. Try for one moment letting go of all the pain and hurt you've received from someone else. Try letting go of all the guilt for the pain and hurt you've inflicted on someone else. See if your slippers are still there. Click. Click. Click. What does the world feel like when you can choose rather than regret? What does it feel like to be Queen?

An Authentic Queen Is A Capable Steward of Her Talents. A Queen spends time determining what her innate talents are. Once she identifies them she spends time accepting and developing her gifts. Then, without hesitation, a Queen takes her God-given talents out to the world.

For some, recognizing and accepting their talents is easy. There are specific slots for their abilities such as singer, dancer, artist, baseball player. For whatever reason, when it came to following their hearts, this group did not let the voices of others or external influences persuade them. For others, uncovering their talents and finding places to use them is a nightmare. My path to self-mastery was the latter. It took years to unearth my talents, potential and courage. And, longer still, to implement anything substantial.

For the latter group, the process can be, and probably is, pure torture. Some Queens, then, understand that they haven't discovered where they fit and are a work in progress. An Authentic Queen doesn't have to have all the answers, but simply needs to be working on it—doing things like studying, researching and exposing herself to a variety of opportunities. She is exploring and will not stop until the hunt is over. Once the search is complete, she will spend her time launching her business or grabbing that job. She will do whatever it takes to use her talents wisely. A Queen recognizes that God gave us gifts to make our hearts sing and to serve others.

A Queen Understands SHE is Her Greatest Potential

Our biggest challenge is coming to terms with our greatness. For whatever reason, we have forgotten that to *be* is powerful. According to the *Course in Miracles*, the biggest challenge to overcome is the belief that the "cause of one's problems is 'out there.'" The key is understanding that nothing external to us can make us happy or not or that "love is not something that is given or taken away by another, but instead is created within."

Culture, opinions of others, and suppression have layered over our authenticity. Probably the most opposition we face is our intellect. Our mind thinks it knows what is real, but it has interpreted reality incorrectly, thus creating confusion, mishaps, and cravings for things that do not serve us. If only we could 'see' our world as God sees. If only our decisions and reactions were based on God's view. Understanding the limitations of our mind, even a Queen's mind, is key to unlocking our highest potential.

Allowing the ebb and flow of the Universe while also accepting it, indicates the need to no longer beg and plead with God. No one knows what is best for oneself. *No one*. All we can do is *think* we know and therein lies the problem. Uncovering our greatest potential, then, is to grasp the meaning of "letting go" and "letting God" while ridding ourselves of cultural and acquired baggage, and setting the highest aspirations for ourselves we can imagine. Although our minds confound our understanding, we must always remember that our dreams lead the way to our greatest potential.

CHAPTER FOURTEEN

Sisterhood of the Queen

The Conscious Queen

I was the Self-Help Queen. I keep looking for the key. But so many of the books I read seemed to focus on how to get bigger boyfriends and better cars. I wanted to know how to find myself.

—Kathryn, 52 years old

I T IS POSSIBLE for every Queen to find her way. I know this from firsthand experience. Some of us will do it early in our lives, some will find their way while approaching our middle years, but most of us will not find our clearly recognized path until we hit our forties, fifties or sixties.

At some point you will stop. You will recognize the pain and confusion you have been experiencing is your Shadow Self, your Unlived Life, calling to you in love. You won't head for the refrigerator or open a bottle of wine. You won't go shopping, or pop that pill. You won't decide you need a 'bigger boyfriend or better car.' You will have found the key to the self you locked away so long ago. She will emerge, bringing with her the joy, peace, and love that has eluded you for all of those years.

When I first began my process, I didn't have a plan. I guess I finally started hearing my Glinda the Good Witch whispering her blessings. Not only did I start to hear her, but I also started acting on *her* promptings. That is when the tide changed for me.

What happened first? How did I start the process? When did I first reach for my tiara?

Without pre-meditated forethought, I decided to form a group of friends. Was Glinda calling from my heart? I had just returned to West Texas, and I only knew one person to contact.

Making the call was very difficult. Kecia, my lone friend, was popular and had more than enough friends in her inner circle. She didn't need me to make her life complete. I needed her more than she needed me, and I didn't like to admit it. If she turned me down, then I had no backup plan. It took me many days to muster up the courage to call her.

"I was wondering if a group of us could form a weekly lunch group, just for fun," I told Kecia. I thought the group should be large—up to fifteen—so when some of us couldn't attend, we'd still have a good crowd.

Kecia loved the idea, but she said, "Let's keep it small. I know two friends that will be perfect! I'll call them."

Quickly, the idea turned into her party because she had the contacts. Our small, intimate group of women friends was born. In hindsight, I recognize we created a safe, cozy place to share fun, sadness, laughter and tears. For about two years, we experienced our highs and lows together. We started with lunch and ventured into girls' weekend trips and New Year's Eve parties with spouses.

The group, without meaning or purpose, opened my heart—the first step towards healing.

Jump forward about four years. I now find myself in a new town with a new team of Queens. Again, my team has no purpose. Well, actually our purpose is to have fun. That's it. That's all we do. Of course, within the structure of having fun, we are building binding relationships.

Love. It comes in all shapes and sizes, outside the family as well as within. And this is what love does. It is the support that holds us steady as we try new endeavors. It is the support that cradles us in times of sorrow. It makes laughter deeper. It helps dreams come true. And when it is given, it increases until it overflows, until we are sharing it with everyone we meet.

Steps to the Queendom—Grabbing Your Queen Power

Step One: Create your own Group.

Quite possibly the realization I had no connections in my new community pushed me to contact Kecia. What if something happened to Greg? To Addy? To me? Who would I call? Who would care? My parents and sisters lived more than 800 miles away.

Alone, I had reached a turning point. My Good Witch Glinda saw an opportunity to whisper to me. Heck, maybe she yelled. No matter, I heard and embraced her message. No longer comfortable with loneliness, I picked up the phone. I made that call. I changed my life.

I highly recommend that you establish a 'social' community, a group for 'fun.' In today's world, where people relocate often, and we are in our cars more than we are on our sofas, it's easy to get 'dislocated.' Gathering with a group of women to have fun—laugh, play and giggle—is the way to open yourself to new and exciting possibilities. Developing friends from work or other activities takes time. One friend who moved a lot in her early adulthood said she discovered it took at least two years to establish intimate friendships and seemed to take longer the older she got. Like everything else, you can speed up a time frame if you add a little structure. That's your Team. You don't even have to wear your tiara, though my group has, and we weren't the only ones who ended up having a good time. The combined energy of good friends is contagious. If you don't have a community now, try it. It is highly recommended that the social group be comprised of women living in your geographical area. It's best if you can hug them on a regular basis!

At a later date, you might also decide to develop a 'Dream' group, a foursome (or more) that has the sole intent of helping all members reach a specified goal. Set aside specific times to meet and discuss goals and activities. I've found two separate groups, one for play and one for goals, are better than trying to combine the two. The 'Dream' team also can be an online group comprised of like-minded individuals residing in various parts of the globe.

Your groups can also have other purposes. One forum, I am particularly fond of, is the Monroe Expand App. You can create your group and share meditations, messages and other information with each other.

When we reach out to one another, we will find the use for the talents we were given. In our groups we learn to receive as well as give love. And we will be fulfilling our utmost purpose on this journey—we will be saying yes to love.

Step Two: Stop the Mean Voice

I know that, like forgiveness, I continue to stress the need to alter your negative self-talk. But, it's most important and worthy of repeating. There is nothing like a bout of self-bashing to make you feel your tiara has slipped for good.

Let me emphasize again—your thoughts create your reality. It really, really is true. If you call yourself stupid, you will meet people who will assist you in believing it. If you think of yourself as willing and capable of learning new things, you will find you are using and increasing the talents you were born with, and that people step forward to give you many opportunities to do so.

Georgia Richardson author of *A Funny Thing Happened on the Way to the Throne*, had this to say: "Practice makes anything easier. Another fact that may help break loose poor feelings is to know: You feel them so easily because you've been practicing feeling them. They're not new to you. You've unwittingly allowed yourself to experience them, *repeatedly*. Be aware that whatever you do repeatedly will become easier and easier to experience, whether good or bad. This is, simply put, *habit*. Remember, no one can get inside your head and make you feel anything. That habit or repeat experience is up to you."

Live a Powerful Life (formerly titled Grab the Queenpower) collaborator and editor Donna Warner, when asked if it were true that we were responsible for our own happiness replied, "No. You don't control your own happiness. That was a gift of grace, which can be obscured but not discarded. You are, however, responsible for your unhappiness, and for taking those steps to see what thoughts are creating the emotion, and for letting them go. Once you have done this 'observation' your natural state of happiness shines through."

It's simply a matter of monitoring your thoughts, and then altering the negative messages you continually utter. Create mantras or affirmations to replace the 'bad' things you say. Transition your thoughts from judgment to acceptance.

It's not easy to change old habits. It took me several years to reach a new place, but with each day, you will draw closer to being a true friend to yourself.

Step Three: Pay Attention to Your Dreams

Learning dream symbolism is a very important step to self-awareness. Recording and evaluating your nightly visions will most definitely get you headed in the right direction. Dreams are messages our subconscious mind sends us while sleeping.

Some of us remember dreams more than others. I'll experience periods of time when I do not remember many, then I'll be hit by a slew of them.

To trigger your memory, tell yourself repeatedly while drifting to sleep that you plan to remember the dreams that have important messages to share. Eventually, you'll start remembering. Although it is fun to believe that dreams are psychic predicators, rarely they are. The majority of dreams are snapshots of our daily lives including struggles, joys and bothers.

Interpreting your dreams can enhance your everyday life and it can also be fun. Once you figure out dream language (symbolism), it seems easier to find meaning and/or guidance.

My first caution is to emphasize that only the dreamer can accurately interpret her dreams.

The second is to stress dream dictionaries are limited in the scope of their assistance. Yes, those resources can and will provide you with tremendous insight, but you must take all definitions for what they are—suggestions by another individual. If a definition doesn't resonate with you, then it's probably not the meaning you are seeking. Sometimes, you'll simply have to let a dream go and 'not' figure it out—especially in the beginning. But, at other times, you will be amazed at what you've learned or uncovered about yourself.

If you are serious about this endeavor, I suggest either purchasing a dream dictionary or accessing on-line dream dictionary resources. To make certain your resource is good, check if it's relatively free of fear-based definitions. Sources that mention words like, "bad omens," or "financial misfortune will befall you" are not good dream dictionaries. Besides being filled with superstitions, this type of resource leans towards psychic predictions.

Keep this one simple rule in mind when starting out. Other people in your dreams usually represent aspects of yourself. Morton Kelsey, author and Episcopalian priest, believed that eighty percent of the time this is the case. After years of interpreting my own dreams, I agree with him.

Here's what works for me: First upon awakening, write down the dream. The sooner you do this, the better. I cannot tell you how many times I have lost significant details because of failing to write the dream down immediately upon awakening.

After you record it, read the dream and see if anything comes to mind—pay attention to emotions such as happiness, joy, sadness, fear. Consider every aspect of the dream. What words or symbols seemed significant to you? Think about this dream I recently remembered:

One of my teeth fell out of my mouth. It fell on the desk where I was sitting. I held it up to examine it. It appeared healthy. Not concerned, I continued working. Later, another perfectly healthy tooth fell out of my mouth. Suddenly, I became quite concerned.

When turning to my online dictionary, I found several definitions that did not seem to apply. For example, one of the sources claimed, "dreaming about teeth is a bad omen that suggests financial difficulties." This is what I'm talking about when I say please use some caution. If you took this symbolism literally, you might be in a tailspin about your impending financial doom. Instead, the part that explained "teeth symbolized power" spoke to me. With the definition understood, my directive was to consider in what aspect of my waking life I was losing power? After additional thought, I actually pinpointed an occurrence the previous day in which I allowed my negative self-talk to rule supreme, thereby allowing me to lose power. Because I am always working on the negative chatterbox that likes to call me names, I got the all-important message from my subconscious mind. It said, "Stop it!"

Interestingly, the repetitive part made me take additional notice, and after I figured it out, I vowed to return to being nicer to myself. Smart move, I think. Who needs to lose power? I certainly don't! See what I discovered? And to think, I have only a dream to thank.

Step Four: Declare your Intent. Prepare to listen and act on inner promptings.

Several years ago, I made the decision to develop a greater awareness of my intuitive nature. Although I have always been highly sensitive to the feelings of others, I wasn't born with an elevated ability to interpret my intuitive whispers. It took practice and time.

The key was trusting myself and acting on the messages I received.

Doing the same will ease the way to utilizing your Queen Power to the fullest.

The next move is to make a pledge. "I promise myself that I will take action based on the intuitive hits I receive." When beginning the process, you are going to miss some of the hints along the way.

That's life, and as is true with any new skill, you must practice. Simply recognize the misstep as soon as possible. Quite frankly, many of your 'hits' are going to blow right over you until you are ready to 'hear' them clearly.

Pay Attention to the Clues Dropped by the Universe. We're often so closed off from our directives that we either don't hear them or completely miss them altogether. To make lasting change, you must make a declaration. By doing so, you are accessing the power of intuition. But, before you do, it is vitally important that you understand with this commitment comes the duty to act. Simply asking to 'hear' more clearly doesn't alter your current situation. It's the acting on the inner promptings that change the course of your life. Glinda is speaking to you. She is reminding you of the silver slippers you are wearing. As Nancy Sinatra so fittingly wrote and sang, these *shoes* (okay, so she actually said boots) are made for walking.

Not stepping out shuts down the inner messages just as much as external noises. If you need support (and courage), form your own group.

Starting is the key. "Turn around. Go to that store. Say hello! Call Jane." Whatever you hear, sense or know (we all experience different ways of communicating with ourselves) accept its value. Don't think your thoughts are crazy or unfounded. If you get the nudge to hug someone, do. If you get the urge to avoid a person, do that, too. Eventually, you'll work up to strong feelings and sensations that either warn or prepare you to take the next move.

I no longer have to guess if I should collaborate with another person or not. Actually, fine-tuning this skill takes all the guesswork out of hiring. It significantly cuts out the need for extensive investigation. Whew! It's something I know simply based on an interaction. I feel a certain way and I have learned to recognize those feelings.

I remember years back when I use to be unnerved by the security guard that regularly checked on our office. Something about him made my skin crawl.

My reaction to his visits prompted me to never stay late without another person around. Although he appeared nice and presentable, on some level I sensed the danger.

Turned out this man had murdered someone. The security company missed this important little fact, but my higher self or inner knowing sensed danger.

Many people, me included, find answers in the quiet moments when your mind is still, and the chatter is minimal. My best time to meditate or contemplate is in the morning immediately after waking up. That's the time when you are the closest to a 'dream-like' state, which is highly conducive for communication with your higher self. Other hints include being open to receiving answers and suggestions. Your messages could come from within or from others. Yes, the Universe uses other people, circumstances and physical sensations to inform you. The main point is to recognize the need to pay attention. Your Queen fairies are all around you, dropping you little, essential hints continuously.

For example of how to pay attention, notice where you hold anxiety. Some people feel their throats constricting while others feel a heaviness in their chests. Anxiety always speaks to me through my stomach. When others are unhappy, depressed or stressed, including myself, my Good Witch Glinda whispers it to my gut. No, my stomach doesn't hurt; it simply feels differently. You've all had a 'hair raising' experience. That's your intuition telling you there's danger.

So, how to we make sure and keep our connection open? We do things like pay attention to our dreams and learn dream language. We stop the mean voice, which also helps us not worry or fret. We forgive ourselves and others. We trust—trust in the process, in the messages and in our ability to do what we are here to do.

Step in the direction of intuition and you will move forward with much more ease and grace. There is one caveat. Fully using the gift of intuition doesn't mean that all decisions and challenges will be easy. What's in your best interest—what guidance is 'suggesting' you do might still be difficult. Asking and receiving verification to add a child to your family mix doesn't necessarily mean the child will be healthy. It simply means that having a child (whether healthy or not) is right for you.

As with all new skills, this one requires much, much practice. The ability to 'hear' your Good Witch Glinda is very real and something you can learn to do.

Step Five: Forgive Others for all the Real and Imagined Transgressions Against You

Okay, as they say back home, I'll repeat this till the cows come home. Forgive. Forgive. Forgive. Holding on to grudges, seeking revenge or stuffing down anger only makes you sad. A Queen will never find the peace and joy she seeks if she hangs on to the injury caused unintentionally or purposefully by others. Truly, it is all about "letting go and letting God." It's a matter of surrendering the 'accusatory' stance and ultimately allowing those feelings to float away. As explained earlier, it took me numerous times to go through the process of forgiveness and actually to experience release. The turning point hinged on finally understanding that most people aren't trying to hurt, but instead are simply seeking to get their own needs met. Sometimes you get in the way and sometimes you get hurt. But, more times than not, the hurting was completely unintentional.

You will also find the more emotional trauma and garbage you clear from your mind, the less hurt and pain you will experience...from others or from yourself.

Forgive. Oh, I feel a must coming on. If you're gonna be Queen, you just gotta do it!

Step Six: Treat Yourself Like a Queen

Have you recognized yet how many of the same qualities that are necessary to claiming your throne are the same ones that keep the tiara gleaming? Repetition is always helpful when you are learning new habits.

Being 'selfish' came easy to me. I worried about it, but did it anyway. I was so into "give me, give me" that I simply felt guilty and ashamed for wanting to take care of myself. Again, I think my low energy level made me act more selfishly than maybe my true nature was comfortable with.

Many women go the other direction and think any need to take something for themselves is an indication that they are self-absorbed. Sneaking away for two hours to nap, read or to be alone would fill some women with a tremendous sense of guilt. "Oh, I really shouldn't have done that. Selfish, selfish, selfish."

Throw in children, chores, work, domestic responsibilities, and extra-curricular activities and you quickly realize how hard it is to find time for yourself. My sister shares the frustrations of being a working mom: "I work full-time, which leaves little time to do all of that other stuff I want to do. Somehow, I've got to reset my priorities and distinguish between what's important and what's not. Most of the time, what happens is that the 'stuff that can wait' is what's important to ME!"

Friend and author Ann Leach along with co-author Michelle Beaulieu Pillen had lots to say about selfcare in *Goal Sisters*: "Selfcare doesn't have to carry a negative connotation. Easier said than believed, right? Consider the following: 1. Being 'selfish' (or rather, taking time for yourself) can also mean taking care of yourself emotionally, physically, mentally and spiritually so that you can be a better mom, partner, friend, employee, sister, aunt and so on; 2. Self-care may mean shifting some responsibilities with grace as you make room in your life to achieve your own goals; 3. Making self-care a priority may improve your relationship with yourself—especially the part of you that walks through life like a robot and the part of you that doesn't know what you want because you haven't given yourself the luxury of ever finding out."

Christine Hohlbraum author of *Diary of a Mother* shared, "As for being 'selfish' to find 'me' time, I find it essential to explore who we are to be able to give to the extreme we mothers have to every day. So no, it is not 'selfish', but essential. If your gas tank is empty, you wouldn't attempt a long car trip, right? It is not self-indulgent to want an hour to ourselves. It is a necessity. How many times have you witnessed parents snap at their children at the grocery store? Do you think it was because they had just gotten a massage or taken a weekend getaway with their partner? No! They are stressed out, worried about money, sleep-deprived or stretched for time. At the same time, it is our responsibility to get what we need. Doing without in the long run serves no one, including ourselves."

If you have something that is your responsibility that really drains your energy, look for a creative solution. As I've already said, I hate housekeeping, and pay to have it done even when I had to scrimp in another area. My energy flows so much better when someone else does the vacuuming and bathrooms for me.

Of course, I do the daily stuff (cleaning the kitchen after cooking and washing clothes), but it's so nice to have someone else dust, mop and scrub the toilet. It frees me from resentment and anger, and then the other things I do don't bother me. I can cook, clean up the kitchen, wash the clothes without feeling a double drain on my energy—doing the chore and resenting the time it takes me to do it. I've found what I can do joyfully, and have given the rest away. So far, the price has been well worth the rewards.

My solution won't work for everyone, but if you remember you are a Queen and turn to your intuition for help, you can design your own life, so your energy is used to its best advantage.

Step Seven: Dream Big, But Take Small Steps

Once you start clearly hearing your Good Witch Glinda, your tucked away dreams will start emerging. You'll hear whispers. Before you know it, a picture will appear. At some point, you will know the direction you *must* go. Turns out it was always the way you needed to go, but since you completely missed it till now, you stumbled. Eventually, you will know where the road is, how to find it and where it will take you. Finding it, you'll start moving closer. One day you'll wake up and realize you are there. One day you'll understand that happiness, joy and peace have always been your right. And it's now yours to share.

Step Eight: Queens Focus

As I worked on writing this book, I made every effort to focus on related tasks, which included writing, editing and promoting. Many times, I got distracted or found myself wasting time on meaningless activities. But no matter, and despite myself, I still devoted *enough* energy to the mission to enable something to manifest.

If you like thinking in angel terms, can you imagine the angels' frustration when they *try* to help us? In deep prayer and with sincere meaning we pray, "Dear God (and angels) help me launch my website for women trying to lose weight." Celebrating, the angels start swirling around their magic dust in that direction. Finally, you have heard the *right* message. Finally, you are heading in the direction of your heart.

A couple of days later, we tell our husband (which just happens to be within hearing range of our angels): "Okay, I finally know what I'm going to do. I'm going to get my real estate license!"

The angels scurry around shaking their heads wondering what else they need to do to get our attention. But, they help us anyway. Knowing full well that in less than six months we'll abandon that pipe dream because it simply doesn't suit us. They figure learning about what we don't want might actually help us return to our purpose. At the end of the six months, sure enough, we are unfulfilled and seek something else. Briefly, we think about what we *really* want to do, but quickly talk ourselves out of it. "I don't have money to launch a website. It's crazy to think that other women would listen to me. I'm too fat to help other women. Yep, just like I thought, the idea is stupid."

Once you start to focus on your path and daily strive towards something that provides meaning to you, you will wonder what took you so long. For me, even on the supposedly bad days when nothing goes right, all is *right* in my world because I'm doing what I am here to do. That's it. A joy that previously eluded me surrounds me, and keeps me grounded even when my external world seems crazy.

If nothing else, understand and appreciate that most people find great reward (and meaning) from helping others. If you can't pinpoint exactly what you are supposed to be doing, then start helping others face-to-face. And, here's a Caroline Myss quote I couldn't resist: "*I rarely meet people who want to retire from a meaningful life.*" Think about it!

Step Nine: Become a Conscious Queen

I want to help you realize that no matter how much money you have, no matter what sex, race or age you are, you do have power. You *can* make a difference in your world and in the life of every single person you encounter.

—Caroline Myss

I regularly think about Emily Dickinson's poem, *Love's Baptism*. In the poem she tells us, "With will to choose or to reject. And I choose—just a throne."

This refrain reminds me that I do have the power to choose, which also means it is my choice to live, or not, a powerful life—a life I navigate and direct. Once you start living more authentically, your power will slowly emerge and begin filling you with light. One day you will awake and find yourself bathed in the glow of personal power. In that moment, you will know that you are truly on your way. You will know from heart to mind that you are where you are supposed to be and doing what you were placed on this earth to do. It's that simple. Of course, that doesn't mean it's necessarily easy.

I look back on my life like a good day's work, it was done, and I feel satisfied with it. I was happy and contented; I knew nothing better and made the best out of what life offered. And life is what we make it, always has been, always will be.

—Grandma Moses

Saving Graces

My aunt was my role model. She had no children when I visited her. I was the Queen. At my home, we had nine children, and my mother always had a baby on her hip. Aunt Dorothy would take me to guitar lessons, water ballet lessons, made doll clothes for my dolls. I was the Queen Bee.

—Vicki, 59 years old

My aunt Kay was my role model as a child, but when I did not follow her path, I forgot to follow her methods. During those *lost* years I longed for a role model, a teacher—somebody to offer me a hand. Help me. Show me how. I felt smart enough, competent enough, but didn't know *how* to make anything happen except for the traditional way that had been modeled to me. Not only did I feel a constant pain—sadness, discontentment—I also struggled with finances. Not one to stick around long in a job, I never established myself and always was paid less than my value, rather my perceived value. With a pressing desire to be free of a traditional life, I floundered as I tried to 'make it' without the benefit of regular income. It took me years to figure that one out.

Again, I did so without the support of a mentor or role model. Not that the media didn't show me plenty of successful women doing things they loved. It was obvious when picking up any magazine that many women have successfully figured it out. My problem was that I couldn't figure out *how* to create in my own life what 'they' seemed to have in theirs. As far as I could tell, I didn't have anyone within reaching distance that could show me how.

Going down the road without a guide turned out being a hard row to hoe, as they say back home. I am convinced my lonely walk ended up being a lot longer than it had to be. By nature I am a loner, but I never found anyone who could seem to understand where it was I was trying to go. There were brief moments when I found mentors, but those times were few and far between. There were also times I found the wrong person, people who caused more harm than good.

183

Out of necessity, I created my own way, forging ahead in unchartered territory. I made many, many mistakes.

In 2000, I started making real connections with other women via the Internet doing the things I was attempting to do. Utilizing message boards and websites, I successfully found woman after woman working in the career/self-help field. Some were willing to briefly correspond with me by e-mail. Others sent out weekly e-zines to inspire me.

No matter, for in this magical world of the web, I found mentors and peers. My world suddenly got bigger, and I started to see new and exciting possibilities. Without the assistance of on-line discussions by members of a national résumé writing association (Professional Association of Résumé Writers and Career Counselors—PARW/CC), it would have taken me years longer to master the business. With my learning curve cut in half, I started making money almost immediately. Finally, with the help of others—others doing what I wanted to be doing—I could see the pieces falling into place.

With all that said, then you'll understand why helping others reach their goals is so important to me. I wasted valuable time and shed too many tears while stumbling through my life.

CHAPTER FIFTEEN

The Language of Dreams

M Y JOURNEY BEGAN so many years ago, before I left the girl/ boy Never Land of childhood. It started with my 'mares… the terrifying dreams I had of The Worms, Go-Fish, and the Hallway. Often in my life my dreams continue to come to me as messengers from a deeper consciousness than I can access in my run run run Red Queen waking life.

Because I feel dream symbolism is so important, and because interpreting this dream clarified my journey and its significance to me, I want to share it with you.

I was on a journey, accompanied by many women. The woman leading us followed directions using a crude map only she seemed to understand, we walked from point to point.

In a quiet neighborhood, our group of diverse women spread out over the yards of two houses. Flowering trees provided us with shade. Children played in the streets. The women milled about, and I was frustrated. I felt we were in danger if we didn't move forward. I felt

because we were so exposed, we must be in danger from someone who wished us harm.

I approached the group leader and asked if some of us could move ahead. She was waiting on something or someone, and could not leave yet. She said we could move on, and showed me the map. It was hard to read. Even though I wondered how in the world I'd reach the next place, I decided to go ahead anyway.

Several of us started out. Along the way I peered into a cave-like room (dark, gray, cold, damp) and thought, I've been here before.
Our leader and the rest of the group caught up with us so quickly, I was surprised.

Together we looked for the next destination. In addition to the map, we had been instructed to look for an oddly shaped building (more dome like than anything) with a large, yellow net hanging off of one side of it. We were told when we found the building to go inside.

With the leader's help, we were easily able to find the building. We went inside to a bar filled with people. They were on a journey similar to ours, and were already at round tables drinking milk out of baby bottles.

The leader approached the bartender. She wasn't sure what to order. It seemed to me that she didn't even notice what the other people were drinking. I pointed them out to her.

She said, "Yes, we'll all take one of those."

When I woke up, I recorded my dream. Several details seemed immediately evident.

The journey to self-integration is not for a few selected individuals. We all are on the journey, male and female. Those of us who are awake, meaning aware of the journey, sometimes get the idea that faster is better. The term *divine timing* comes to mind. In my dream, the leader wasn't ready to move ahead yet. She, the part of me closest to my heart, needed more information and guidance.

In my haste, I made erroneous assumptions—one, that we were in a race and two, that by exposing ourselves we were in danger. Neither scenario was true. In fact, by listening to external advice I was off the mark. I felt the external advice was the messages I had received from my culture.

I left early following a map I didn't have the means to understand. My departure from the group took me by the cave-like room. A damp, dark, cold place filled with sadness and loneliness.

Remember my thoughts upon peering into the room? "I've been here before." I peered in, lingered for a little while, thereby losing time. While the leader waited in a nice, safe neighborhood with trees, children and dogs, I passed the time in a dark, damp cave. I couldn't wait for divine timing. I didn't trust my inner voice would know when to go. I had to push to move forward.

The leader and remaining members of the group caught up with us before we reached our final destination. I wanted to ask, "How did you catch us so quickly?" In my head I heard the leader respond, "With the new information I obtained after you left, I was able to take a direct path. You left before getting the final instructions. The map you read was garbled, unclear."

Reaching the final destination, we made our way to the dome-like structure marked with a yellow net. I remember thinking how easy that part of the journey seemed. We were suddenly right there.

According to an on-line dream dictionary I frequently use, www.dream-moods.com, I discovered that entering a dome symbolizes honor—celebration of success. Reaching our destination was a cause worth celebrating.

And what about the yellow net? Nothing I found in the multitude of sources out there resonated with me, so I thought about what a net means to me. Immediately, I thought of safety, as in safety net. My group, then, entered a safe place. It later occurred to me that in this case, yellow is symbolic of the harmonic convergence of love (heart), courage and intellect.

By entering the building we had reached the next level of transformation—an integration of heart, courage and intellect—and had much cause to celebrate. Admittedly, I was somewhat confused by the all-important destination point being a bar. My first thought was it might symbolize celebration. However, I found comfort in additional information collected in another on-line source: www.dreamloverinc.com. According to Silvana Ivin-Amar, school psychologist and author of the web site: "When I was in college, I read in a theology book that a monk on a mountain top and a man with his bottle of wine are really trying to get to the same place. That 'place' translates to peace and a genuine feeling of being connected to the rest of the universe. Dreaming about being in bars and drinking may symbolize a need that you have for some type of a meaningful transformation." The bar symbols our need for transformation and our desire to be closer to God.

Thinking about the significance of drinking milk was puzzling to me at first. All the patrons were drinking milk and we, too, ordered milk. According to Ms. Ivin-Amar, milk signifies that "your unconscious mind may be suggesting that it is time for you to grow and to learn and that it is possible for you to do that at the current time." She also states, "Drinking milk suggests a renewal in spirit and thought, just like springtime is the renewal in nature."

Interestingly, the leader (my inner guide) wasn't sure what we wanted, and it was up to me to point that out to her. I think I was required to make the choice to signify the concept of *free choice* or *free will.* Remember, I was also allowed to take a detour earlier even though my inner guide (leader) knew I was going off course. No matter this dream tells us, the destination will be reached, even if you can't read the map or don't listen to intuition. It's easier if you do, of course, but not a requirement. It's simply a matter of time—divine timing.

In the dream, we were there to drink the milk—to have our journey mean something. Ordering milk was the rite that marked that phase of the journey complete. Just like all the others at the bar, we wanted and ordered milk. Happily we drank the milk, signifying our willingness to nurture our feminine aspects, thereby celebrating our renewal in spirit and thought. We had (all of us in that bar) reached a destination point and it was cause to celebrate—we, while raising our bottles of milk, toasted change. Our trek had been long, our path winding, but together we paid tribute to our great work knowing in time we would be rewarded.

Round tables also have significance—to see a round table in your dream indicates evenness, sharing, cooperation and equal rights and opportunities for all. It may also symbolize honesty, loyalty, and chivalry.

All the details in a dream have been chosen by the subconscious to inform the dreamer, and the significance of the details must resonate with the dreamer. Paying attention to dreams yields the same rewards as paying attention to life…if you do so, you will more quickly discover where your purpose is leading you.

CHAPTER SIXTEEN

Hands Reaching Out

Dream Excerpted From My Journal

I saw myself climbing a muddy hill. I was struggling, but finally made it. Many voices were calling to me from below, "Help us, help us, help us get over this hill." I found myself at the top, and the hands of others had reached down to help me get there.

I SO OFTEN FELT my life had been one following a long and twisting road. Along the way there were sometimes minor bumps and curves, and gently sloping hills. But much of the time there were mountains and mudslides. I was grasping. I was slogging. At those times it felt I was getting nowhere.

Gradually the landscape began changing. I could feel myself changing. I wanted to know why my life became difficult, why I often felt so lost, such despair. I wanted to clearly examine the process of awakening to my Self—to becoming who it felt I was supposed to be. The biggest challenge in this journey toward self-awakening was that I didn't personally know anyone else who seemed to be experiencing the same thing. One friend was on a spiritual quest, but our paths appeared so different. We could and did support one another, but neither of us could show the other *the way* to get to our unknown destination. Without a lead or guide, I often stumbled.

This project started because I desired to understand what happened in my life. My initial idea was to dig deeper—deep enough to find out what happened to me and to so many other little girls.

It is my desire to help our daughters by-pass some of the trauma we adults have experienced. I want to provide a new female role model so grandmothers, mothers, aunts and friends can alter some of the ancient rules about what being a woman means. Together we can write a new chapter in our culture. We can create a world where both girls and boys thrive, where each gender does not have to be alike unto itself, but can develop talents and skills that are different, and are valuable in that difference.

I decided in order to advance these ideas, I needed to write a book. Even though an experienced grant writer, I had no luck securing grant dollars to help fund my efforts. I researched writing opportunities and checked out ways to make money while I pursued my *real* project. I held onto my part-time day job, and I was able to dabble in writing—to play writer. During this time I started *talking* about my project and interviewing relatives. I still couldn't call myself a writer. That would take much longer. But I could tell people I was interested in talking to women about their lives.

At first I had no idea what I was looking for, though I had vaguely targeted gender issues. I actually called the work I was doing the *Gender Project*. I pondered, read and studied until my book began to take shape. I interviewed more women, and then conceived of the idea to get help from even more.

I realized I needed to employ a more official process, effectively expanding my subject list with the help of Dr. Dorothy Jo Shawhan, Delta State University (DSU) English Department Chair and published writer. Dr. Shawhan discussed the project with her writing students. Several expressed interest and agreed to visit with me. With a forty-question format, tape recorder and appropriate releases, I visited with each student for at least two hours. The interviews were fascinating. Still with no clear purpose, I continued to gather data.

Approximately one year after I started gathering oral histories, Dr. Elizabeth Sarcone, English Professor of DSU, recruited students to do additional interviews. At the time I was living in Texas, more than 800 miles away from the subjects, and needed help gathering the data. With the assistance of her students, twenty-two interviews were collected.

The best interviews for my understanding were the ones I did. Content was not the sole source of information. Subtleties helped shape my story. By observing the interviewee, I learned much about her and her life.

In the beginning, the questions highlighted gender differences.

Specifically, the subjects answered questions about childhood and motherhood. In an attempt to maintain structure, I directed the student interviewers to ask the same questions. Basically, the women were asked to share what it was like growing up, purposely discussing how they were treated as compared to their brothers, male cousins or male friends.

By the time I finished the process, I had interviewed over twenty subjects personally, and student assistants had collected seventeen usable interviews. In the summer of 2004, I finished up by collecting ten more. In the last round of interviews, the subject 'talked story' and I simply listened.

Most of the subjects were born and raised in Mississippi. Only a few were born in surrounding southern states with the majority residing in Mississippi for most of their adult lives. The ages spanned from 20 to 100 with nearly all of the included interviews ranging in ages from 30 to 80. The most common age ranged between 45 and 60. Two-thirds of the subjects were Caucasian, and one-third were African Americans. Although about half of the subjects did not have brothers, all had male cousins or friends to use for comparison purposes.

Many people who wanted to share their experience were uncomfortable about being publicly identified. For this reason, I used a pseudonym or changed some identifying biographical information.

To help the subjects relax, the interviewers asked basic information about their lives, such as where they grew up and currently lived. Another light-hearted question asked interviewees to think of southern sayings they heard while growing up. Many of the answers were amusing as well as insightful. A woman that grew up on a farm in rural Mississippi shared the funniest one I heard, "Keep your legs crossed so your Christmas won't shine." Many shared commonly used quotes that served to shape our cultural ideas about raising children, specifically girls.

Thus my 'Gender Project' began.

As I collected my information, I included quotes from authors whose books were informative about my subject matter. I began 'hearing' voices speaking about women and their concerns. From television programs to articles in magazines, other voices—women's and men's—called out, each with something important to say. I have included many of those quotes in *Grab the Queen Power,* and credited the source when I had one.

I began my journey thinking I was alone. My journey is far from over, and I am far from alone. "Help me," I used to cry out in despair. Help has come. For that I am forever grateful. It is a privilege of those who have received to extend those gifts to others. This book is the gift I was given. I am now giving it to you.

EPILOGUE

And They Lived Happily...
One Day At A Time

Getting started is the hard part: Inertia works positively and negatively. When you're stuck in your life, it takes a lot of effort to get unstuck. (It took me more than a year to work up the courage to begin writing the first story of *Defying Gravity*.) But once you make the effort and start going in a new direction, it's relatively easy to keep on going.

—Prill Boyle

As a NAÏVE five-year-old who didn't know I wasn't going to be myself, I was the champion of the underdog. I took on any tormentor. I believed in a good world, and if someone else didn't, I was determined to set the transgressor to rights.

I ran away from the spindle that claimed Sleeping Beauty. No domesticity for me. As far as Snow White's apple—thank you, I had already had my plate of tuna for the day. And Cinderella—ask me to mop for those

195

stepsisters, and I would have thrown ashes at them. Anyway, my prince and I went to high school together, and he would have accidentally broken any glass slipper.

But that Wizard. That little old sham. I jumped right into that hot air balloon, and it's taken me many years to figure out what direction is home.

I believe the opportunities we are not given are as great a gift as the ones we are given.

—Kathryn, 52 years old

What I have discovered was I've been headed home all the while. Looking back over my life I've discovered I've had a use for every part of it. The fearless little girl/boy ready to take on the world. Yes, I needed her. I still do.

Mrs. Ousley, who told me I couldn't be Queen. In order to be Queen, I had to create a map for myself, forge the tools to fashion my throne. Like Dorothy's companions, I had to learn Mrs. Ousley couldn't make me Queen. I had to discover I had always been Queen by using the qualities that define what a Queen is.

The bleak years of junior high school were necessary, too. They taught me my instincts were right even though my world told me something else. Braving the hurricane wasn't easy and I had so much trouble coming out. But, enduring those thorny times proved something to me. I was resilient. I could fight back. I could survive.

In college I learned what I was *not*. I learned that the epitome of social success doesn't substitute for purpose in life. And the sorority taught me any number of skills of working with groups of people with different and exacting personalities.

My undergraduate degree in psychology has fueled my interests in the way we move and change in the world. The MBA developed my organizational abilities, and certainly has helped me in my goal of being self-employed.

Each step that didn't work was a step toward one that did.

Beginning with my 'mares, as a child, dreams have foretold and deepened my understanding. As I turned toward the home of my childhood, collected the voices that taught me what I needed to say, and continued my own journey toward wholeness, my dreams came to me in the language of symbolism, showing me where I was heading.

The vibrant sky complimented the deep blues and greens of the ocean. Standing on rocks warmed by the sun, I took a deep breath before diving in the cool, crystal-clear waters. Today, I planned to swim with dolphins. A new experience, I found it impossible to contain my joy. Swimming out to the contact point, I took in all the sights both under and out of the water.

Upon arrival, I waited for the dolphins to join me. I kept waiting and nothing happened. After a short while, I started sensing the danger. What was I thinking? Seriously? Here I was alone surrounded by deep, dark water and who knows what underneath. I panicked. Before completely losing control, I remembered thinking, "Hey! Wait a minute. This is a practice drill. I can immediately return to the shore. All I have to do is wish it so." I closed my eyes and made my desire known and suddenly, I found myself on the rocks.

Consider the symbolic meaning of the dolphin. A dolphin typically indicates our readiness and skill to navigate through our emotions. In the case of starting out in the direction of your dreams, one must be able to work through fear—a powerful and limiting emotion. Recall the dream, suddenly and without warning fear snuck up on me. "What am I thinking? Am I crazy? Who knows what big scary man-eating monsters are swimming down below? How can I get back to where I started? Stupid! Stupid! Help me!" Sound familiar?

Aren't dreams grand? When fear consumed me, I was able to shout, "Do-overs!"

In the next phase of the dream I decided to hire a guide.

Finding a line of people, I waited patiently for my turn. Eventually, though, I moved forward and reached the counter, a place to find help. Once at the counter, I explained my intent. The lady selling the tickets tried to talk me out of it. "It's very dangerous. The place they take

you is covered by a cliff of rocks and the guide can't see you while you swim." Determined to reach my goal, I could not be dissuaded. I said, "No, I'm doing it. Yes I will be afraid, but I am doing this."

Again, the symbols of dream language spoke volumes. Standing in line points out the need for patience. Like in your waking life, you take small, careful steps in the direction of your desires while spending time waiting for results to manifest. It takes time to reach your destination. Deciding that I needed a guide—ah, finally I was ready to listen to my heart, my inner self, I stood my ground. As evidenced by the lady at the counter, following your heart never *appears* safe and in fact can be dangerous, risky and unpredictable.

But don't forget the words of Caroline Myss: "The safe path is the *real* illusion." Yes, the path you perceive is out of harm's way is anything but. The key is to remember the promise that when you listen to your Good Witch Glinda your silver slippers will always protect you, even if the way seems filled with monsters, big-sea creatures and brutes.

Ready to move forward, I suddenly realized I didn't have my purse with me. I had no money. Promising that I would be right back, I fled the hut and started on the long journey home. Heading in the right direction, I passed by some men hanging out on the beach. Frightened by their words and actions, I decided to go home the back way—the safe path. I climbed over steep rocks and trudged through mud. While stopping to catch my breath, I looked at the path ahead. Filled with more mud, high grass and deep water, I determined I didn't want to work so hard anymore and returned to the sidewalk. Despite my fears, I returned to the well-traveled road and walked the remaining journey with ease.

Interestingly, according to dream dictionaries, a missing purse indicates that you may have lost touch with your real identity. When considering the dream and the message of this book, I must make a connection. For so long, I had gone along with the path laid out before me—the one that took me away from my self, away from the traditions that had always comforted me. So, to get my purse (basically to return to myself), I had to take yet another journey. Again, fear sidetracked me and made me take the long, arduous and trying path—this time it was represented by men. And in this book I have explored those patriarchal rules, which made the traditional path seem the dangerous one for me. Therefore I had to leave the familiar path, and take what appeared to be a more difficult, unmapped one. But, as I returned to my real identity, I gathered strength and overcame my fears. I plodded on until finally fear was not enough to keep me on the difficult road. In the end, I returned to the sidewalk—the traditionally walked path. But this time and after releasing my fears, my journey home (to my authentic self) turned out to be joyous, peaceful and fun, and without barriers.

Dolphins have become a powerful symbol for me as I sought my 'right life.' When I watched the movie of the 'dolphin lady' as she worked with wondrous animals, I suddenly knew what my 'right life' would feel like. That was only a piece of the puzzle, but this one is now in place. I have the life I wished for so many years ago. And, always, the path leads on…

The most exhausting thing you can do is to be unauthentic.

—Anne Morrow Lindbergh

Growing up, I was always exhausted. I simply did not have any energy, and always had to pace myself. The more I listen to my inner voice, my Glinda, and follow her instructions, the more energy I find I have. The wrong path will sap your energy until you cannot go on. Then you must find a better way. When you do, you will be provided with all the energy you need.

As I worked toward completing the book, and I had another dream:

It was time to go. I announced to a group of women, "I'm driving!" As I marched around to the driver's side of the car, I remember thinking what a great car this is. It was silver, sporty with a hatch door. I gleefully said, "Wow! I'm driving Cat Woman's car." I jumped in and squealed off. And as I quickly sped away, growled as only Cat Woman could do.

No need for any Wizard and a simple hot-air balloon headed in the wrong direction. Talk about energy. What could be more powerful than a silver CatMobile? Wearing my silver slippers, I had upgraded. And I was taking my friends with me.

The psyche is not so much a mechanism as a weaver of narratives. We do not tell stories only: we are stories.

—Craig Chalquist

We must be careful of the stories we tell ourselves. When I realized the story of the Princess no longer fit, it opened the way for me to begin the new story, the one of the Queen. I felt my new title required recognition. I dislike ceremony, and usually avoid participating in manmade ritual. But having named myself Queen, I felt the need to designate my throne. After all, if I didn't, who would?

I had to decide what my throne would look like. Where would I put it? Somehow a jewel-encrusted monstrosity in my living room fitted neither my lifestyle nor my pocketbook. I am somewhat a simple Queen.

My throne is simple, too. It's my straight-backed wooden desk chair. Nothing fancy, really—just a chair.

Trying to decide on a ceremony for my throne made me wonder, though, how do you know it's time to name your throne? At what point do you become a Queen—someone worthy of even having a throne? As I thought about this, I realized that my transition from powerless to powerful was not immediate. It took time and involved many steps—missteps, side steps, backward steps—steps that stopped off in dark, damp caves and poppy fields—steps that brought me joy as well as anguish. Blundering through most of it, I found some direction from books, friends and happenstance. In hindsight, I realized how much quicker my trip would have been if I'd had a discernable map.

If I ever go looking for my heart's desire, I'll never go any further than my backyard. Because if it isn't there, I never really lost it.

—Dorothy, *The Wizard of Oz*

So I have created one. As I wrote this book, I taught myself. I found my path taking unexpected turns. As I learn more, I am sure my path will change even more. Even as I close this last page, I am thinking…"Wait, I needed to tell them this." And so I will, taking my next step and my next one. I share my map with you, my friends, my

Sisterhood of Queens. I hope it eases your journey. I hope you let me know the secrets you've learned as you've come to claim your own throne.

The ceremony? Mine is simple, too. I pick up my scepter, tap it three times, tap tap, tap, around my simple little writing chair. And, after that I click, click, click my silver slippers.

But first, I have forgotten something!

I run to my closet, in my very own room. There it is. It's been there all along. I pull out my tiara, and place it on my head.

Ah yes, it's good to be Queen.

I done said enough.

—Helen, 81 years old

THE END

The Parable Continues: And, She Lives Happily Ever After

ITHIN THE TIME the Princess worked with the Royal Advisors, she learned many, many things. The Princess excelled and fulfilled her requirements by the end of her 15th year.

On the day the training was completed, the Trumpeter trumpeted, and the Court Announcer announced.

"Your Royal Highnesses today marks the fifteenth birthday of your daughter, the Royal Princess. Today her training will end."

Trumpets resounded. Members of the Royal Court cheered. The doors to the royal chambers were thrown wide open. Flanking each side of the Princess, the three highly ranked Royal Officials escorted the Princess front and center.

The Royal Subjects gasped. The Princess looked like a Queen! Later, they discovered that she also acted like a Queen. She knew exactly what to do and how to do it. The Princess was ready to play her role. All rejoiced including the Queen and King. That evening a birthday celebration was held.

Daily in the chapel, the Queen Mother thanked her God for changing her daughter. "What a gift you have given me. What a gift."

But, as the days turned into months and the months turned into years, the Queen Mother realized her precious daughter rarely smiled. The light and airy steps of childhood were gone.

The Princess often cried, or stuck out her lip. Everyone remarked on her sighing. She couldn't remember if you poured milk for the Royal Cat, or placed the Royal Cat in the milk larder. On a really bad day, she broke the cat bowl. She performed only when she was sure of praise, or for royal frocks and dripping jewels. Countess Corridor, Prince Scarlet and Countess Pride wearied of the young Princess's incessant need of council over every detail, no matter how insignificant. And always she glanced down, never meeting anyone eye to eye.

Years passed by. The Princess never married. Many suitors approached the King, but none ever caught the fancy of the Queen-in-Waiting. The Queen Mother and King Father grew older. One-by-one her teachers grew sick, old and gray, leaving the Princess more and more to herself. She retreated into silence.

On her 40th birthday, the fragile old King and Queen assembled the Court.

The Trumpeter trumpeted and the Court Announcer announced.

Your Royal Highnesses today marks the 40th birthday of your daughter, the Royal Princess.

The Royal Advisors tottered in.

"Why?" asked the King. "Why hasn't my daughter chosen a Prince? Why hasn't she produced Royal Heirs? Why will she sit alone, the last on this Royal Throne?"

The Advisors had no answer.

All the court regarded the Princess. At that moment she herself realized she knew the answer to the questions her King asked.

"What shall I want? What shall I love? What shall I be?" she asked the Royal Advisors. She turned to the King and Queen, the parents who loved her more than life itself. She held out her hands, turning her empty palms upward, but she stared at the ground. Then she said, "I've forgotten who I ever was."

Wringing their hands, the Royal Advisors turned in despair to the King.

"What shall we do?" the King cried.

The Queen Mother at last understood. She, too, knew the answer to hard questions. She stood up and straightened her tiara. "Royal Trumpets, resound," she commanded.

The Royal Trumpeters trumpeted. The Royal Announcers announced, "Here Ye, Here Ye ..." But then, they were confused. What were they expected to say next?

The Royal Queen herself spoke. "I proclaim forthwith I shall sell all the gifts I have received from the Kingdom. I bequeath the proceeds to my daughter. She will take all that I have received and go to seek her Self."

The Royal Court gasped. The Royal King gulped. The Royal Advisors fanned themselves.

At first the Royal Princess looked befuddled. "Will it be dangerous?" she asked.

"Probably," the Royal Queen answered.

"Will I get lost?" the Royal Daughter inquired.

"Very likely," said the Queen.

"Why must I?" the Royal Princess said.

"Because it is your Self that will be found. And all the future depends on it."

The Royal Princess looked her mother in the eye. Then she grinned. She bowed deeply, then stood. "Make it so," she said. And with a flutter of her hand she took her leave, knowing soon she'd experience the world. But she found the most comfort knowing that one day she would return.

THE END

APPENDIX A

Long Live the Queen!

OU'VE DECLARED YOUR intention. You are steadily moving into your personal power. Go ahead. Name your throne. Make or buy queenly items to adorn your throne—your personal space. Purchase and wear a tiara! In my home-office space, I have pictures of tiaras, a Mary Engelbreit 'Q' statue, a scepter and other queenly things. My decorations and adornments are constant reminders of my goal and purpose.

Even my daughter Addy knows about the importance of celebrating in a Queenly fashion. For Mother's Day she once gave me a Mary Engelbreit Queen journal and colored a crown with the inscription: 'Queen Mom.'

With confidence move forward—the answer to all of your struggles is to step confidently towards your Self. Revel in all your glory. Yes, name your throne!

For more information about visit: www.allynmitchellevans.com

APPENDIX B

———————⟨⟨⟨⟨⟨⟩⟩⟩⟩⟩———————

Selected Resources and Recommended Reading

Abbott, Shirley. *Womenfolks.* New Haven and New York: Ticknor & Fields, 1983.

Altea, Rosemary. *You Own the Power.* Perennial Currents, 2001.

Barrett, Michele. *Women's Oppression Today: The Marxist/Feminist Encounter.* (2nd edition) Verso, 1988.

Borysenko, Joan. *Guilt is the Teacher, Love is the Lesson.* Time Warner Company, 1990.

Boyle, Prill. *Defying Gravity.* Emmis Books, 2004.

Course in Miracles, Workbook for Students (Foundation for Inner Peace, 1985.

Dyer, Wayne. *The Power of Intention: Learning to Co-Create Your World Your Way.* Hay House, Inc., 2004.

Estés, Clarissa Pinkola. *Women Who Run with the Wolves.* New York: Ballentine, 1992.

Gilligan, Carol. *In A Different Voice: Psychological Theory and Women's Development*. Harvard University Press, 1982 and 1993.

Hawkins, David. *Power Versus Force*. Veritas Publishing, 1998.

Hawkins, David. *I: Reality and Subjectivity*. Veritas, 2003.

Hillesum, Etty. *An Interrupted Life: The Diaries of Hetty Hillesum 1941 to 1943*. New York: Washington Square Press, 1981.

Hulme, Keri. *The Bone People*. Penguin Books, 1986.

Kidd, Sue Monk. *The Dance of the Dissident Daughter*. HarperSanFrancisco: Imprint of HarperCollins Publishers, 1996.

Knapp, Caroline. *Appetites: Why Women Want*. New York: Counterpoint, 2003.

Lerner, Gerda. *The Creation of Patriarchy*. Lerner, 1986.

Lamott, Anne. *Traveling Mercies: Some Thoughts on Faith*. New York: Anchor Books, A Division of Random House, Inc., 1999.

Maushart, Susan. *WifeWork: What Marriage Really Means for Women*. New York: Bloomsbury, 2001.

Milgram, Stanley. *Obedience to Authority: An Experimental View*. New York: HarperCollins, 1983.

Miller, Alice. *The Drama of the Gifted Child*. Basic Books, Inc., 1981.

Myss, Caroline. *Sacred Contracts: Awakening Your Divine Potential*. Three Rivers Press, 2003.

Myss, Caroline. *Invisible Acts of Power: Personal Choices That Create Miracles*. Free Press, 2004.

O'Halloran, Susan and Delattre, Susan. *The Women Who Found Her Voice: A Tale of Transforming*. Innisfree Press, Inc., 1997.

Orenstein, Peggy. *School Girls*. New York: Anchor Books, Double Day, 1994.

Pipher, Mary. *Reviving Ophelia*. New York: Bantam Double Day Dell, 1996.

Sarton, May. *The House by The Sea*. New York: W. W. Norton, 1977.

Ward, Sela. *Homesick*. New York: Reganbooks, 2002.

Williamson, Marianne. *A Woman's Worth*. New York: Ballantine Books, 1993.

Wiseman, Rosalind. *Queen Bees and Wannabes*. New York: Three Rivers Press, 2002.

Woodman, Marion. *Consciousness Feminity, Interviews with Marion Woodman*. Inner City Books, 1993.

Woodman, Marion and Mellick, Jill. *Coming Home to Myself: Reflections for Nurturing a Woman's Body and Soul*. Conari Press, 2000.

ABOUT THE AUTHOR

A LLYN EVANS, MBA, is the Chief Executive Officer of the Monroe Institute, a nonprofit research and teaching organization dedicated to improving people's lives through the advanced study and practice of expanded consciousness.

Before being named CEO, Allyn served as the Chief Program Officer. After four months of serving in this role, she was asked to serve as the Interim Executive Director, which eventually led to the permanent appointment she now serves. Allyn became a residential trainer for the institute in 2011. Her training assignments included the flagship introductory Gateway Voyage program based on the work of Bob Monroe as well as OBE Spectrum, also offered at Monroe. An energy healer, she continues to train Energy Medicine. She creates and voices meditations for programs at the institute and the new Monroe Expand App.

One of Allyn's favorite annual trips is going to the Bahamas and swimming with dolphins in the wild.

ACKNOWLEDGEMENTS

It takes many hands to make a book.

Oh, to remember all those who have been instrumental in the birth of a book!

—Carolyn Howard-Johnson

THIS BOOK IS so close to my heart because it's about the stories of our lives. Although every effort was made to give credit where credit is due, it is very possible that in this process someone was missed. More specifically, concerted efforts were made to discover the ownership of all copyrighted works and to secure the required permissions. If any printed work is questioned and found to be inadvertently included, the author and publisher will be happy to make the necessary corrections in additional printings.

Thanks to my dear friend Margaret Staton for planting the seed.

It takes many more hands to help create a story.

Donna Warner, my editor and collaborator—who started as an interview subject, then later helped me find others to interview—was instrumental in helping get this work put together. The project pulled her in. Next came the editor's hat. Highly skilled, Donna helped me transform stories, interviews, ideas and practices into written words making the message clearer and stronger. Donna also had a little of her own story to tell and so her voice, at times, blends with mine as we speak our truths and share. What I'll never forget, though, is Donna's encouraging words and commitment to the project.

Without the help of the women I interviewed, the book's power would be diminished. Thank you for your time and willingness to share private details and stories about your life.

www.ingramcontent.com/pod-product-compliance
Lightning Source LLC
Chambersburg PA
CBHW062138280526
45788CB00001B/213